Regardless of where you li
theologian. Therefore, it is vi... ....p.... .. ...
divorced from missions but is the fuel that drives all missionary gospel
endeavors. In *Missions by the Book*, Alex Kocman and Chad Vegas weave
together a thoroughly biblical argument for why all missionary efforts and
practice must have a comprehensive theology at their core. Missionaries,
students, and pastors alike will benefit from this clarion call to restore
theology to its rightful place.

Dustin Benge | Associate Professor of
Biblical Spirituality and Historical Theology,
The Southern Baptist Theological Seminary, Louisville, KY.

Some books lay out the foundational biblical teachings that must guide
our missionary labors. Some books bring the sharp edge of God's Word to
contemporary controversies in missions. Remarkably, this book does both!
Highly recommended for missionaries, pastors, and all who care about
fulfilling Christ's Great Commission.

Dr. Joel R. Beeke | President,
Puritan Reformed Theological Seminary,
Grand Rapids, Michigan

Missions by the Book may well become the standard text on God-honouring,
Bible-shaped gospel mission to the thousands of unreached people
groups scattered throughout the world. Kocman and Vegas challenge the
methodology of many mission groups that downplays Scripture as regulating
how we are to take the gospel of the God of grace to all the nations. Without
denying the powerful, present ministry of the Holy Spirit, *Missions by the
Book* seeks to take seriously the transgenerational wisdom of God's Word in
understanding how the church today is to seek to reach and win the lost in
every age. The addition after each chapter of a series of questions makes the
book an ideal resource for churches as well as individuals to study this most
vital of gospel imperatives. I commend this work without reservation.

Ian Hamilton | President,
Westminster Presbyterian Theological Seminary,
Newcastle, England

Missions and good theology began as good friends but have gone through a rocky period the last sixty or so years. All manner of lone-ranger missionaries, speed-based methodologies, and bad hermeneutics have found great traction in the present missions world. Vegas and Kocman have brought back a refreshingly clear and biblical understanding of our Triune God's desire and plan for all nations. It is my fervent hope and prayer that it is embraced widely by pastors, Christian leaders, and those who will take the gospel of our Lord to the ends of the earth.

Brooks Buser | President, Radius International

MISSIONS
BY THE BOOK

MISSIONS BY THE BOOK

HOW THEOLOGY AND MISSIONS WALK TOGETHER

CHAD VEGAS AND ALEX KOCMAN

CAPE CORAL, FLORIDA

Missions by the Book

Copyright © 2021 by Founders Press

Scripture quotations are from the ESV® Bible (The Holy Bible, English Standard Version®), Copyright © 2001 by Crossway, a publishing ministry of Good News Publishers. Used by permission. All rights reserved.

Published by

Founders Press

P.O. Box 150931 • Cape Coral, FL • 33915

Phone: (888) 525-1689

Electronic Mail: officeadmin@founders.org

Website: www.founders.org

Printed in the United States of America

ISBN: 978-1-943539-29-1

All rights reserved. No part of this publication may be reproduced, stored in a retrieval system, or transmitted in any form by any means, electronic, mechanical, photocopy, recording or otherwise, without prior permission of the publisher, except as provided by USA copyright law.

Cover Design by Perry Brown

Typesetting by InkSmith Editorial Services

Contents

Acknowledgments v
Foreword ix
Introduction 1
Chapter 1: The Word of God as the
Sufficient Authority for Missions 9
Chapter 2: The Father's Decree to
Send the Son to All Nations 21
Chapter 3: The Son's Mission to Save All Nations 31
Chapter 4: The Holy Spirit's Mission as
Witness to Christ in All Nations... 45
Chapter 5: The Church Christ Is
Building in All Nations... 57
Chapter 6: The Apostles' Commission to
Proclaim Christ in All Nations.. 75
Chapter 7: The Nations and the Church's Commission........ 87
Chapter 8: The Power of Ordinary Gospel Preaching 107
Chapter 9: The Glorious Reward in Missions 119
Chapter 10: The Missionary
Commissioned to All the Nations 135
Conclusion 147
Appendix: The Apostolic Evangelistic Preaching Pattern .. 153
Bibliography 155
Scripture Index 161

Acknowledgments

Behind every meaningful Christian book are deep supply lines of family members, colleagues, spiritual leaders, and committed friends whose championing of the authors made the publication possible. This book is no different. As with any work undertaken for the Lord, putting pen to paper—or finger to keyboard—is a labor of love undertaken in dependence on the grace of God and the support of each part of Christ's body. We are deeply indebted to each person whom the Lord used to help make *Missions by the Book* a reality.

We want to start by thanking men like Carl Trueman, Ian Hamilton, and others who encouraged Chad, a preacher at heart, to distill his theologically grounded approach to missiology in written form. Men, without your encouragement and exhortations, we would not have come to this point. We also give thanks for the many people who read our chapters and provided feedback. Thank you to Richard Barcellos, James Dolezal, Josiah Vencel, Vanessa Dotinga, Benjamin Vrbicek, and the missionaries of Sovereign Grace Church. We thank Peter Sammons at The Masters Seminary and Tom Ascol at Founders for inviting Chad to teach on missions, which gave rise to this book. Moreover, we thank God for our wives, Teresa and Hanna, whose forbearance with our busy schedules, additional reading, long phone calls together, and extra time withdrawn in our offices enabled us to persevere.

From Chad:

Teresa, through all the many twists and turns the Lord has carried us through as we travel the King's highway toward the Celestial City, you have been a constant encouragement and companion. You are an excellent wife, a grace to me from the Lord.

To my elders and deacons: I can imagine no greater joy than serving Christ and his church with you men. Apart from your co-laboring in the gospel, I would lack both the strength and time to accomplish much. You brothers are often the grace of God that strengthens me to continue to fight the good fight.

To Jason Faber: I can imagine no co-laborer in the ministry more godly, faithful, and wise than you. I often get the public recognition, but you are the man whom the Lord has used to shape Sovereign Grace and keep her steady in ways others will never know or see. The Lord knows. I know. My family knows. We love you, brother.

To Brad Buser: The Lord brought you into my life in 1999, and I have never been the same. He used you to open my eyes to God's heart for every tribe, tongue, and nation. The Lord has allowed our work together to start a training organization that has been growing quantitatively and qualitatively, despite our own foibles through the years. I am thankful you were willing to take a backseat to your son, Brooks, as he leads us forward. Your humility in doing so has been a gift to Radius.

To Alex: Thanks for taking my call and agreeing to help with this project. You are a better writer than I. I am privileged to have you along for the ride. I pray our efforts are a blessing to Christ's church.

From Alex:

Hanna, I'll never forget how when the moment this opportunity arose, you replied, unflinchingly, that I had to undertake this work because it was what my life up until this point had been aiming toward. Thank you for your kindness, grace, and the countless hours of care for our children—not to mention the child born during the writing of this book—that you sacrificed to the Lord to support this ministry.

To my parents: I owe you my humblest gratitude for cheerleading my writing efforts all through my childhood. Every good parent tries to encourage their children's natural abilities, but you meant every word of praise. Yes, you were hopelessly biased, but God used your affirmation in my life, nonetheless. You always said I would publish a book. Here you go.

To Chad: Thank you for the invitation to be a part of this project. Your zeal, intellect, and devotion to this work have been both a source of spiritual strength to me and rebuke of my sloth. I have seen the fruit of your ministry through the men of your church and the graduates of Radius International—it's the real deal. May the Lord continue to bless you in all the work you undertake.

To Scott Dunford: Thank you for your mentorship, your deep thinking about missions, and your friendship. You never regarded me as just a mobilization prospect but always as a brother. As much as I've learned from your heart for the nations, I've learned even more watching you lead your teams, navigate workplace issues, love your wife and children, and shepherd your flock. We've served and fought side by side, and when we disagree, we sharpen each other. I thank the Lord for you and for the ABWE family, which brought us together.

Finally, both authors thank our Triune God for his electing love, redemptive work in Christ, and rescuing power through the Spirit by which we stand today. We are not worthy to participate in his mission, much less to write or think deeply about it, yet he has called us and "qualified [us] to share in the inheritance of the saints in light" (Col 1:12).

Foreword

Missionaries live in the cross-pressured environment where the doctrinal nature of Christianity, with its claims to truths that transcend specific times and places, meets the evangelistic nature of Christianity, where the need to communicate the faith to those outside the church is paramount. And tying those two things together is not, and never has been, easy. How do we confront the cultural status quo in a manner that makes the offense of preaching that of the gospel and not simply that of the missionary's own cultural tastes and preference? And how do we communicate the gospel in a way comprehensible to those being evangelized without reducing the gospel simply to their own cultural tastes? That is the challenge of Christian missions.

This is one reason why Christian missions has at certain points in history been the dynamic for the subversion of the faith. In the early twentieth century, J. Gresham Machen correctly identified the presbyterian missions as the epicenter of practical theological downgrade, epitomized by the work of Pearl S. Buck. And what Machen identified then as a problem has only grown in significance since. As the wider culture of America has moved further and further away from anything resembling the moral imagination of generic Christianity, we are all, so to speak, on the mission field now. We all wrestle with the cross pressures that were once the preserve of those our churches sent to far-off lands. The problem of the practical connection of doctrine and life, of theology and proclamation, of conviction and strategy, are pressing issues for every congregation and every believer.

In this context, this book is helpful on two fronts. It works beautifully in terms of its stated objective, that of reflecting on missions in light of the above tensions. But it also works as a fine reflection on all our lives as Christians in a cultural environment that is increasingly alien to our view of the world.

The basic question is this: Does theology drive practice, or does practice drive theology? That is a missions question with implications well beyond the mission field. It connects to how we address homosexuality and sexual mores, for example. It connects to how we assess the usefulness of non-biblical approaches to the world around us. It connects to how we think about the gospel in a post-Christendom age. For these reasons and more, this is a significant book to read and consider. Simply written yet profound in the thoughts and discussions it will no doubt stimulate, it is something for us all to ponder, and having pondered, to apply.

Carl R. Trueman
Grove City College
July 2021

Introduction

When was the last time you wept over a theological document?

After nearly a quarter-century in the corporate world, Alan[1] and his wife existed in luxury and ease and attended a casual, entertainment-driven church—living out their American dream. But when they encountered the biblical doctrines of grace—grasping that "by grace you have been saved through faith . . . [a]nd this is not your own doing; it is the gift of God" (Eph 2:8)—they realized that their lives were not their own. At the same time that they stumbled upon the theology of the Reformation, they also recognized their missionary call. They put themselves under biblical teaching and were sent to Africa to reach Muslims with the gospel in an international city. As they deepened in their understanding of Scripture, they became convinced that it was the task of missionaries to patiently establish healthy, organized, doctrinally rich churches. This led many of Alan's more pragmatic colleagues to dissociate from them, convinced Alan and his wife had become imbalanced fundamentalists unwilling to properly adapt their church traditions to the local culture. Discouraged yet undaunted, Alan continued to build inroads into his community and began discipling a former Muslim—now a Christian—in leading his church plant.

In a series of meetings with the up-and-coming pastor, Alan decided to teach through a historic confession of faith. As the missionary expounded an Arabic translation of the confession, the African pastor was brought to tears. "The first missionary who discipled me over twenty years ago taught me all these truths," he explained. "Then, for

---
1 Pseudonym used to protect this missionary's identity.

the past twenty-plus years, numerous missionaries have told me these doctrines were not true. I don't know what to believe!" he lamented. During another study session, the pastor lay facedown on the floor and cried out to the Lord for clarity in front of Alan. Many previous missionaries had failed to instruct the man in sound doctrine, teaching only a series of Bible stories and life lessons, robbing the new pastor of the richness of Christian tradition. Yet through Alan's ministry, this began to change.

Have we, like Alan, allowed our theology to overwhelm us with a sense of our indebtedness to the lost and unreached? Or, like Alan's colleagues, have we seen the plight of the lost and opted for quick fixes, reserving the best biblical teaching and theological resources for ourselves?

There is a crisis in evangelical missions. A great gulf is fixed between the realm of theology and the world of missions. On one side of the rift, those who most love theology fall prey far too easily to pharisaism, intellectualism, and apathy, keeping them from the front lines of missions. Young men pursue theological degrees, compete for a small handful of available ministry jobs to pay off their school debts and support their young families, settle into routines, and wake up decades later inside the evangelical cultural ghetto. On the other side of the rift, many of the most adventurous, risk-taking mission workers are trained to check their theology at the door of their sending organization and learn a host of man-centered ministry tactics that stem from cultural relativism. These missionaries are told that the same gospel-centered, doctrine-rich teaching that builds faithful churches in the West won't work elsewhere in the world and that some new and different insight from sociology is needed in non-Western cultures.

When we fail to savor and apply our theology, a lack of zeal for missions is never far off. Simultaneously, those most zealous for missions often look on historical theological tradition with suspicion. In short, bad theology leads to bad missions, and bad missions spreads more bad theology.

We, the authors of this book, were not immune from this unbiblical way of thinking. In college and early in ministry, we both came from the "theologian" side of the gulf. We were both well-read enough in the Bible to craft spiritual-sounding excuses to ignore missions but not steeped enough in Scripture to feel the weight of Christ's call to the nations. We both had a litany of reasons why we weren't called, gifted, or required to serve the nations in some way—reasons we found persuasive at the time. We were painfully awakened in our twenties to our own apathy and the ordinary Christian's obligation to the cause of the gospel across the globe. We became haunted by the roughly two billion image-bearers of God careening toward hell without any access to the gospel. Later, we were called into youth pastor positions in our respective churches and eventually found ourselves involved in missions, not primarily as goers but as senders: Chad through founding Radius International with Brad Buser and Alex through becoming director of missionary mobilization and communications for the Association of Baptists for World Evangelism (ABWE).

Through these parallel journeys, we both became aware of the great need for missionaries—and of a temptation plaguing the missions community. We, like many, feel the pull of sacrificing truth on the altar of expediency. Yet in much of modern missions, theology and practice are readily and unbiblically divorced from one another. We often hear that Scripture does not necessitate any one particular method in ministry, that matters of methodology are neutral. If the method "works"—by bringing about conversions or at least interested seekers who consider themselves obedient followers—then the method is considered to be ordained by God. These "new measures" are christened a fresh wind of the Holy Spirit, even if their practice lacks biblical support.[2]

But does such thinking really affect ministry on the ground? Indeed, it does. To pick an example close to home, we ourselves see the fruits

---

[2] "New measures" is a reference to the new methods that Charles Finney employed in the Second Great Awakening, which he claimed were more effective than the more traditional—and biblical—means employed by the church. For more on this, see the helpful book, Iain H. Murray, *Revival and Revivalism* (Edinburgh: Banner of Truth, 1994).

of such pragmatism in the North American church growth movement. Sadly, generations of church leaders have built organizational empires by promoting a theologically shallow, entertainment-driven model of worship. Then, when the attendees of such churches are revealed as false converts years later, few make the logical connection necessary to call into question the initial methods used to build such ministries. We, too, feel the pull of evangelistic urgency that often drives the seeker-driven or "attractional" church. Yet time has shown that shallow outreach produces shallow Christians.

Astute observers often recognize the dangers of pragmatism in a domestic ministry context, yet those same observers miss it entirely when it manifests on the mission field. For a variety of reasons, we seem to believe that overseas missions, particularly in difficult places, is so mysterious and extraordinary that its methods thereby fall outside our ability to critique. This is often driven by genuine humility and deference to self-sacrificing missionaries who seem to know better, and such humility is often commendable. But it is simply untrue that the average believer or church leader, Bible in hand, is unequipped to exercise discernment in matters of cross-cultural missions. The biblical methods of Christian ministry are the same anywhere in the world, from the U.S. to the jungles of Papua New Guinea. No matter where one goes in the world, the Bible is the word of God, and the God of the Bible is God. Every people group on the earth is made up of those who are sons of Adam, no more or less guilty and corrupt in sin than we are. In every corner of the earth, Jesus still occupies his throne, his atoning work avails to forgive sin, and his sole mediation brings man to God. Regardless of the language, culture, worldview, or skin pigmentation of a people group, the Holy Spirit works in them in the same way. He applies the work of Christ through the ordinary declaration of the Word to every tribe, tongue, and nation.

It is true that cross-cultural ministry is unique. Missionaries must become adept in language learning, cultural adaptation, translation, literacy, church planting, and business-as-mission in closed countries. They will face trials such as culture shock, marital conflict, and child-rearing stress and may encounter disease, infestation, inferior medicine, governmental challenges, and even persecution. Missionaries may be marginalized, threatened, ejected from a country, imprisoned, beaten, harassed, shamed, or legally suppressed. These harsh realities *rightly* make us slow to judge our missionaries, who pay so high a price and should be honored. But none of these realities alters the foundational principles of gospel ministry. And to hold forth these principles, the church is responsible to ask hard questions of those we send.

The central contention of this book is that Christian doctrine and missions methodology must *walk together*, hand-in-hand. Our ministry tactics always derive from what we really believe. Hence, methods are not a matter of liberty but fall under the express prescriptions of Scripture.

At root, this thesis is simply an application of what theologians have named the *regulative principle* to the church's missionary task. In the context of public worship, the regulative principle is that Scripture's teachings, explicit and implicit, *regulate* church practice. Thus, worship should involve such things as congregational singing, prayer, reading and explanation of Scripture, preaching, confession of sin, fellowship, and observance of the sacraments, as these elements are explicitly put forth in biblical teaching. This differs from the *normative principle* some hold, which maintains that Scripture merely *norms* Christian worship in the sense that what is not explicitly forbidden may be practiced. In this model, impressionistic painting or dance performance could be included in the church's public worship since they are not explicitly prohibited. But we hold, as a rule, that Scripture is to regulate (not merely norm) the practice of the church and that this rule applies to missions as much as it does to worship. Within this, we also recognize that Scripture gives the people of God enormous liberty in every area of life, including both worship and missions practice. We savor this freedom in Christ! Yet our aim is not merely to find the outlines of biblical missiology so we may freely color within; rather, this book is meant to draw out what Scripture clearly prescribes for missionary activity and build on this foundation.

By treating missions in this way, we believe we are putting the power to "do" missions back where it belongs: in the hands of ordinary missionaries, churches, pastors, and believers. Anthropology and sociology have valid insights to offer. But if missions leaders lean on these disciplines such that ordinary believers see the missionary task as lofty and inaccessible, we have not honored our Lord. Instead, we believe that because the Word of God regulates and prescribes the missionary task, everyday believers (like us!) can be a part of God's exhilarating work in drawing the nations to himself.

We also intentionally selected the phrase "walk together" with respect to theology and missions methods to reflect the work of the Dutch Reformed theologian Petrus van Mastricht (1630–1706), who penned the following words:

> Theology must be taught according to a certain method, and it must be the kind of method in which theory and practice always walk in step together. In fact, they must walk together in such a way that theory precedes and practice follows in every one of theology's articles. . . . By this method, I say again, practice should be joined to theory, not only in the whole corpus of theology, in such a way that the first place is especially reserved for the things that must be believed and the second for the things that must be done, but also that in each member of theology, practice should walk in step with theory in a continuous agreement.[3]

We all agree that faith and life are inseparable. So are theology and missiology. Apart from sound doctrine, one cannot have healthy missiology. Doctrine determines practice, and practice always betrays doctrine. The New Testament bears this out. The apostle Paul believed and argued this very thing. He was pressed by the Corinthian church to engage in the superior methods of the so-called super apostles who were drawing large crowds. He rejected their worldly methodologies with extreme prejudice (1 Cor 1:17; 2:1–5; 2 Cor 2:17; 4:1–2; 11:12–15). The ensuing chapters will seek to follow the pattern of Paul as we ground our missiology on the truth of biblical doctrine.

---

3 Petrus van Mastricht, *Theoretical-Practical Theology, Volume 1: Prolegomena* (Grand Rapids: Reformation Heritage Books, 2018), 67–69.

We have framed this work as an address to missionaries, present and future, and to the churches, leaders, and laymen who sustain them with their gifts and prayers, to the end that they would all behold and cherish the gospel truths that drive our mission. We feel the pull, like many, to rush off into activity without immersing ourselves in biblical teaching. We also personally feel the danger of not allowing these teachings to reshape our affections. So, we write not merely to fill the head but to fill the heart to overflow in word and deed.

To that end, we are also writing for men like the African pastor, starved of the richness of Christian heritage. We are writing for the countless national preachers, teachers, missionaries, and ordinary believers laboring to know deeply a Christ previously foreign to them. We are writing for the persecuted church leaders of Asia leveraging the web for biblical resources to supplement training of underground seminaries. We are writing for the faithful women who minister in Islamic lands where sexes segregate and Christian women are left alone to answer the most challenging apologetics questions posed by Muslim women. We are writing for the generation of children who, to our shame, have read few missionary biographies. And we are writing for the ordinary believers at home, faithfully giving and praying yet unsure of which workers to support, why, and how. In all these cases, it is our prayerful expectation that simple delight in divine truth will thrust our readers out on mission with boldness.

Our prayer is that this book would serve as a trusted resource for your ministry, whether you are one who goes to the field or one who sends. You don't need a degree in missiology to faithfully invest your life overseas or discern what you see happening abroad. The Word of God, alone and in its entirety, is sufficient to equip goers and senders for the entire missionary endeavor (2 Tim 3:16–17). We must simply let our faith and our practice walk together.

1

THE WORD OF GOD AS THE SUFFICIENT AUTHORITY FOR MISSIONS

All Scripture is breathed out by God and profitable for teaching, for reproof, for correction, and for training in righteousness, that the man of God may be complete, equipped for every good work.
2 Timothy 3:16–17

"You have so much in English; we have so little in Bengali."

It was 1968. These heavy words, spoken by a Bangladeshi woman named Basanti Das to an American missionary lying ill with a mysterious virus, hung in the thick, humid South Asian air. The Baptist mission worker, Jeannie Lockerbie, had no more than arrived when she fell ill, along with all but five of her teammates. Some were bedridden and quarantined for as long as eleven months. Basanti, a schoolteacher and translator, had come to visit Lockerbie and was eyeing her impressive bookshelf.[1]

Basanti's lament haunted the missionary. William Carey, known as the father of the modern missions movement, had built his ministry in the Asian subcontinent around Scripture translation and the establishment of a printing press. Yet 175 years after Carey's landfall,

---

[1] For the full story, see Loren Skinker, "All Things for Good," ABWE, published July 13, 2020, https://www.abwe.org/blog/all-things-good.

Bengali believers still faced a biblical and theological famine. Once she recovered, Lockerbie began a literature ministry, and the team committed to translate the New Testament into the language of the nearby Tripura tribesmen. When the translation was finished, the tribal chief told the missionaries, "Now that we can understand the Bible, we have no excuse not to obey."

God does his saving work in his world through his written Word. The accomplishment of God's mission depends on Scripture being read, understood, and proclaimed in the heart languages of peoples from all the nations. This is what the framers of the Westminster Confession of Faith meant in 1647 when they noted that the Bible is "to be translated into the vulgar [that is, common] language of every nation unto which they come, that, the Word of God dwelling plentifully in all, they may worship him in an acceptable manner; and, through patience and comfort of the Scriptures, may have hope."[2]

Yet in our era, even Christians are tempted to question the centrality of Scripture. In the United States, a prominent evangelical multisite church pastor, whose weekly attendees total more than forty thousand people, preached in 2018 that we must "unhitch" ourselves from the Old Testament and argued that the maxim "'for the Bible tells me so'. . . is where our trouble began."[3] Similar problems plague the mission field. Translations of the New Testament only outnumber translations of the whole Bible (both testaments) by about 2.6 to 1.[4] Worse, a growing number of Muslim Idiom Bible translations (MITs) intentionally remove or redefine terms like "Son of God" in an effort to encourage Muslims to "convert" to Christ without transgressing the formal boundaries of Islamic religious identity.[5] Wherever we turn, the

---

2 Westminster Confession of Faith (henceforth WCF) 1.8.
3 Andy Stanley, "Aftermath, Part 3: Not Difficult // Andy Stanley," YouTube, 39:44, April 30, 2018, https://www.youtube.com/watch?v=pShxFTNRCWI.
4 United Bible Societies, "About Us: Incredible Growth in Scripture Translation," UBS Translations, United Bible Societies, accessed July 25, 2020, http://www.ubs-translations.org/about_us.
5 One example is the "translation" titled *The True Meaning of the Gospel and Acts in Arabic*, ed. Mazhar Mallouhi (Beirut, Lebanon: Dar Al Farabi, 2008). This translation, for instance, butchers Matthew 28:19's injunction to "[baptize] in the name

Bible is under attack—even from within the ranks of Christian workers. Yet we cannot even begin to approach the missionary task without a rich understanding of and reverent awe for the written Word of God.

THE CENTRALITY OF SCRIPTURE

For much of church history, from the early centuries of the church through the medieval period, Scripture was largely inaccessible. With the exception of the Vulgate, Jerome's Latin translation of the Bible from the fourth century, the Word of God was only readily accessible by an elite, educated few. But the dam began to break through the sacrificial efforts of proto-Reformers like William Tyndale, John Wycliffe, and their spiritual heirs, the Reformers. They were convinced that for the kingdom of Christ to spread salvation to every nation, tribe, and tongue, as promised in Revelation 5:9 and 7:9, the written Word of God needed to be available in the primary language of the average man. Tyndale wrote, "It was impossible to establish the lay people in any truth, except the Scripture were laid before their eyes in their mother tongue."[6]

The invention of the movable-type press and the value the Protestant Reformation placed on God's Word marked a turning point in the availability of Scripture, and the modern missionary movement starting in the eighteenth century opened the floodgates of global Bible translation as never before. At the onset of the nineteenth century, Scriptures were available in just 68 languages; now, Scriptures are available in at least 2,479 languages, with 451 languages possessing entire Bible translations—a 3,546 percent increase.[7] It is no wonder that Christianity has grown explosively throughout the Global South in

---

of the Father and of the Son and of the Holy Spirit" into "cleanse them with water in the name of God and His Messiah and His Holy Spirit." See David Harriman, "Epilogue: Force Majeure: Ethics and Encounters in an Era of Extreme Contextualization," in *Muslim Conversions to Christ*, eds. Ayman Ibrahim and Ant Greenham (New York: Peter Lang, 2018), 491.
6 William Tyndale, *The Works of William Tyndale* (1848; repr., Edinburgh: Banner of Truth, 2010), 1:394.
7 United Bible Societies, "About Us."

the last several decades.[8] God's work in the world is inseparable from his Word. After all, "faith comes from hearing, and hearing through the word of Christ" (Rom 10:17).

God has spoken—decisively, infallibly, to all peoples, nations, and tongues in the written Word of Scripture, which contains both the message and model of ministry. The missionary task is impossible apart from a consuming passion for the Word of God and submission to its authority. But before we can explain the missiological implications of this, we must understand what the Bible *is*.

Two Kinds of Revelation

The Westminster Confession (1647) and the Second London Confession of Faith (1689) both begin their systematic outline of Christian teaching not, as one might think, with the existence of God but with their doctrine of Scripture. The latter confession, to which the authors of this book subscribe, reads:

> The Holy Scripture is the only sufficient, certain, and infallible rule of all saving knowledge, faith, and obedience, although the light of nature, and the works of creation and providence do so far manifest the goodness, wisdom, and power of God, as to leave men inexcusable; yet are they not sufficient to give that knowledge of God and his will which is necessary unto salvation. Therefore it pleased the Lord at sundry times and in divers manners to reveal himself, and to declare that his will unto his church; and afterward for the better preserving and propagating of the truth, and for the more sure establishment and comfort of the church against the corruption of the flesh, and the malice of Satan, and of the world, to commit the same wholly unto writing; which maketh the Holy Scriptures to be most necessary, those former ways of God's revealing his will unto his people being now ceased.[9]

---

8 Sun Young Chung and Todd M. Johnson, "Tracking Global Christianity's Statistical Centre of Gravity, AD 33–AD 2100," *International Review of Mission* 95 (2004): 167; cited in John Morgan, "World Christianity Is Undergoing a Seismic Shift," *ABWE Blog*, ABWE International, June 27, 2019, https://www.abwe.org/blog/world-christianity-undergoing-seismic-shift.
9 Second London Confession of Faith (henceforth 2LCF) 1.1.

These statements serve as the foundation for the rest of the confession. We have a *revelational epistemology*—that is, we know what we know because God has revealed it. In an era of subjectivity in which "truth" is relative, shaped by one's cultural perspective or group identity, we can have unshakable certainty—not merely because of reason or sense perception but because the Author of truth has broken in from the outside and spoken an objective, understandable word. The Particular Baptists in London and the Westminster divines knew that apart from establishing the centrality of revelation, the task of theology is impossible. So, too, is the task of missions.

To this end, God has given us not just one "book" but two: creation and Scripture. The created order is God's *natural* or *general revelation* to us. The framers of the Second London Confession refer to "the light of nature" because they recognized that the truth, beauty, and goodness of the cosmos scream of the reality of the glory of God. David testifies in Psalm 19:1, "The heavens declare the glory of God, and the sky above proclaims his handiwork." The apostle Paul tells us that God's "invisible attributes, namely, his eternal power and divine nature, have been clearly perceived, ever since the creation of the world, in the things that have been made" (Rom 1:20). This general revelation extends from the cosmos all the way down to the individual human conscience, as every human made in the image of God possesses God's unchanging moral law stamped on their hearts (Rom 2:14–15).

Often, when the importance of foreign missions is debated, the question is posed: "What about the man who lives alone on a remote island who has never read the Bible or heard the name 'Jesus'—will he be saved?" This question assumes that either man is only accountable to God if he has been first evangelized or that natural revelation itself contains all the knowledge necessary for salvation. Both assumptions are false. With regard to the second assumption, we should note that the problem with natural revelation is not a problem with the information God reveals but with us, its recipients. In creation, we receive enough knowledge of God to condemn us but not enough to save us. We see the majesty, holiness, and power of God and recognize our guilt and insufficiency, but by stargazing we can learn nothing of Christ, his cross, or his kingdom.

Because we cannot be saved through what we know of God in creation, God has also given us *special revelation*—his spoken, written, intelligible word. Throughout human history, this has consisted of prophetic speech and inspired writings, which have now been finalized with the coming of Jesus Christ, the ultimate Prophet (Heb 1:1–2). Penned by about forty authors over some 1,500 years in three languages and on three continents, the Bible does not represent a single culture's narrow perspective on religion but a concrete testimony from God delivered consistently throughout history to all nations and peoples. The purpose of this special revelation is to reveal Christ (John 5:39; 1 Pet 1:10–12), conform us to Christ (2 Pet 1:3–4), and make us "wise for salvation" (2 Tim 3:15). Scripture, written by holy men carried by the Holy Spirit (2 Pet 1:21), is thus our sole and infallible rule of faith and practice. It is no wonder that David exults, "The law of the LORD is perfect, reviving the soul; the testimony of the LORD is sure, making wise the simple" (Ps 19:7).

The missionary imperative is a direct result of the fact that God has spoken decisively to all peoples, cultures, and times. The transcendent God has made himself known in the Bible. We believe; therefore, we speak (2 Cor 4:13). The question is, how do we speak? Are we free to retool and contextualize our message using any means, assuming those means are not sinful? Or are there also *particular* methods prescribed for us in that very Word?

BEYOND INSPIRATION

Many of us are familiar with the apostle Paul's statement to Timothy that all Scripture is *inspired* or "breathed out by God" (2 Tim 3:16). Note that it is Scripture (*graphē*) itself, the end product of revelation, and not its authors that is referred to literally as "God-breathed" (*theopneustos*). It is not the case that Scripture is merely inspired in the aesthetic sense, just as we might describe an oration or concerto as inspired. Neither is divine inspiration located merely in the redemptive events that Scripture describes, as though the authors of Scripture, weighed down by their cultural and historical baggage, had merely left us an imperfect recording of inspired events and truths we must mine for contemporary application. Rather, the very words they wrote—even down to the grammar and syntax—were the result of the Holy Spirit's superintendence.[10] And because the Spirit does not fail in this regard, Scripture is not only (1) inspired but (2) *infallible*, or incapable of affirming anything untrue. God cannot lie (Num 23:19; Titus 1:2). Further, he is able to communicate above and beyond the initial intention and intellect of Scripture's human authors (1 Pet 1:10–12). This means that the sixty-six canonical books of Scripture are also inerrant—that is, they do not err. Building on this foundation, Paul reminds Timothy that all of God's Word—without exception—is "profitable for teaching, for reproof, for correction, and for training in righteousness" (2 Tim 3:16).

But Paul is not just concerned with abstract arguments about the origins of our Bibles. He is zealous for the missionary task, and his instructions to his protégé concern his methods of ministry. So, in verse 17, Paul continues by explaining that Scripture is inspired "*that* the man of God may be complete, equipped for every good work" (emphasis added). Have you ever sensed your own inadequacy in ministry, whether you were sharing the gospel, preaching a sermon, or counseling a fellow church member over coffee? Paul here reminds us that Scripture itself contains all that the "man of God" (a callback to an Old Testament euphemism for "prophet") needs in order to discharge his mission. Peter makes a similar statement, telling us that "all things that pertain to life and godliness" are available to the believer through the knowledge of Christ (2 Pet 1:3), which comes to us through the text

---

10 This is what theologians refer to as *verbal, plenary inspiration.* Our recognition that the original autographs of Scripture contained the exact words purposefully inspired by God is one good reason to reject such hyper-contextualized renderings of Scripture as the MITs addressed earlier in this chapter. Since God spoke the actual words of the text of Scripture, then faithful translation must stay as close to original wordings and meanings as possible.

of Scripture (vv. 19–21). The Spirit uses his Word to cut to the heart, revealing motives and laying consciences bare before God (Heb 4:12; Eph 6:17). Scripture is not only (1) inspired and (2) infallible but also (3) *sufficient* to equip God's people for his mission.

To say that Scripture is sufficient is not to say that frontlines gospel workers should not learn language, culture, professional skills, or other key strategies for surviving missionary life. The Bible gives us "all things necessary for [God's] own glory, man's salvation, faith and life."[11] It does not tell us how to speak Swahili, change a flat tire while stranded on a dirt road, or balance a checkbook. Such practical knowledge comes to us as God also blesses his people with insight through the realm of common grace. Yet the Holy Spirit has given us his Word as a sufficient resource to enable us to fulfill the Great Commission by his power, disciple the nations through the spread of the gospel, and teach total obedience to the lordship of Christ. We do not gain the necessary edge in ministry by availing ourselves of the latest trends or self-help techniques or theories from psychology or sociology. We do not gain an advantage by playing fast and loose in our translations of the Bible for new languages or audiences, tiptoeing around unpopular words and ideas. With the Word of God in hand, men and women of God are sufficiently armed for every good work.

A fourth characteristic of Scripture must be addressed. The written Word of God is not only (1) inspired by the Spirit of God, (2) infallible, and (3) sufficient but as a result is also (4) necessarily *authoritative*. The problem in contemporary missions is not that evangelical missions thinkers and workers do not affirm the life-changing power of the Bible's message or the importance of translating that message into the heart language of every people group. The problem is that we have not submitted to the Word ourselves.

---

11 2LCF 1.6.

SUFFICIENCY MEANS AUTHORITY

"Marry the mission; date the model."

I (Alex) still remember my reaction when I first heard this maxim uttered by one of the leaders of our large, multisite church, where I served in student ministry. I chuckled, noting the double entendre, but inwardly I hesitated. Our mission, so the thinking went, was to spread the gospel message by any and all means apart from sin; the "how" was negotiable. The logic was appealing. But if this counsel would fail in marital affairs, how could it apply to the bride of Christ?

This pragmatism is rampant within evangelicalism in the West and in the U.S. in particular. The problem is our failure to recognize that God has given us both his *message* and his *means* in his Word. The Word of God not only contains the content of our message to the nations but is our infallible authority regarding the methods we are to use. Paul Washer, president of HeartCry Missionary Society, made this observation at a 2019 conference on missions:

> We cannot have confidence in any ministry unless it is specifically, . . . prescribed by the Scriptures, no matter how noble that ministry may be; if it's not prescribed by the Scriptures, we're in trouble. . . . Throughout biblical history and church history, if there is one thing that God's people, as a whole and individuals, are prone to do, it is this: "And everyone did what was right in their own eyes." In the absence of inspired, inerrant, infallible authority, man will invent. . . . The state of modern missions proves that our great need is to return to the Scriptures. Contemporary mission work is afloat in a labyrinth of contradictory opinions regarding the nature of the Great Commission, the definition and duty of a missionary, and the methods or strategies that are employed. Never in the history of the church have there been so many widely divergent views and such radically incompatible strategies. Such confusion is irrefutable evidence that we are once again guilty of doing what is right in our own eyes.[12]

---

12 Paul Washer, "2019 G3 Conference — Paul Washer — Session 12," YouTube, 1:11:23, February 18, 2019, https://www.youtube.com/watch?v=fJq1xxk1Go0.

Missions strategy, unmoored from Scripture's explicit instructions and example as to the means of ministry, is presently awash in a sea of methodologies drawn not from divine revelation but from such spheres as the social sciences and the business world. We are not free to experiment. We are bound to the Word.

APPLICATION

So, if Scripture is to be our authority, how does it tell us to go about our task? We will return to this foundational question throughout this book, but note these initial observations regarding the role of Scripture in our mission:

1. The Word of God is *supreme*. The Lord Jesus regarded the historic Scriptures as *God's direct speech* to his contemporaries, challenging the Jews, "Have you not read what was said to you by God?" (Matt 22:31). After the resurrection, Jesus sought not only to persuade his followers by presenting the proof of his physical body but also exegeted the Scriptures for them, to open their minds (Luke 24:17, 45–47). The apostle Paul followed in turn, warning the church in Galatia to weigh even the words of apostles and angels against the biblical teaching they had received: "But even if we or an angel from heaven should preach to you a gospel contrary to the one we preached to you, let him be accursed" (Gal 1:8). We must conclude that the Protestant emphasis on *sola Scriptura*—Scripture alone as the highest authority—is not the mere by-product of early modern European cultural controversies but is the clear example of Christ and his apostles.

2. The Word of God is *effectual*. The Spirit of God works through the Scriptures to perfectly accomplish whatever he intends to accomplish in the heart of the reader or listener (Isa 55:11), to open or harden the heart (1 Cor 1:18; 2 Cor 2:14). The Word of God, thus superintended by the illuminating, regenerating, and convicting work of the Holy Spirit,

is powerful and potent as a two-edged sword (Heb 4:12; Eph 6:17), and by it we are born again (1 Pet 1:23; Jas 1:18) and continue to receive our nourishment in the faith (1 Pet 2:2; 1 Tim 4:13). The Spirit's work is so inextricable from the written Word of God that the English Puritan theologian John Owen commented, "He that would utterly separate the Spirit from the word had as good burn his Bible."[13] There is therefore no replacement for reading and understanding the Bible personally for oneself in one's own tongue.

Since God has spoken in Scripture, his Word must be treated as our ultimate, sufficient authority in the way we go about our mission. And if we care about God's heart for the world, we will care that the world has access to his Word. While Scriptures exist in languages spoken by 90 percent of the world's population, more than half the planet's languages and dialects are still without the Bible.[14] Critical work must be done to take the whole counsel of divine revelation to unreached people groups who do not have access to God's Word in their heart language.

As we continue our study of the core doctrines of the faith and their bearing on the missionary task, if we do not first understand the supremacy and power of the Word of God, we will falter right out of the gate. We can only dare to proclaim God's way of salvation in Christ to the nations, at risk to ourselves, because God has cut through the subjectivity of human opinion and philosophy and spoken finally and decisively in a book. Our call to the missionary endeavor begins not with wanderlust or a private experience of calling but with a humble recognition that we hold in our fragile hands the searing words of the eternal God, and he intends for that Word to be read, understood, translated, preached, interpreted, and obeyed. Pick it up and read it!

---

13 John Owen, *The Works of John Owen*, ed. William Henry Goold (Edinburgh: Banner of Truth, 1965) 3:192.
14 United Bible Societies, "About Us."

Study Questions

1. What does it mean to say that God's revelation in the natural realm and in Scripture is the foundation of true knowledge? What are some other sources of knowledge believers tend to rely on instead?

2. What are the two types of divine revelation? What must an individual receive and believe to be saved?

3. What is meant by the terms "inspiration," "infallibility," "inerrancy," "sufficiency," and "authority" in the context of the Bible? In your experience, do evangelical Christians tend to forget any of these doctrines?

4. How should Christians use the Word of God as the final standard for determining issues of methodology? Can you think of particular passages in Scripture relevant to the way we go about ministry?

5. The Westminster and Second London Confessions both state that Scripture must be translated into the common languages of all the nations among whom the people of God find themselves. Why is this? What do you think missiologists mean when they speak of a person's "heart language"?

6. Advocates of the Muslim insider movement methodology promote Bible translations that leave out phrases like "Son of God" so as not to offend or confuse Muslim readers. Why is this problematic?

7. Reflect on your own spiritual journey. How has the Bible affected your walk with the Lord? What would your spiritual story look like if you had no access to the Bible?

8. How does God work in the world through his Word? What can Christians do to help more people have access to God's Word?

2

THE FATHER'S DECREE TO SEND THE SON TO ALL NATIONS

For God so loved the world, that he gave his only Son, that whoever believes in him should not perish but have eternal life.
John 3:16

As I (Chad) sat at breakfast with my friend Emad, we vigorously debated who God is. Emad is a Sunni Muslim who spent much of his life as an emir (local leader) in the city where I live. He is also a vigorous apologist for Islam. Our private breakfast debates have spilled over into a public debate on the nature of God.[1] Emad confesses belief in a unipersonal God, Allah. I confess belief in the Trinitarian God, one God in three persons. Our differing views of God lead to quite disparate understandings of how God works and saves.

I remember distinctly our first point of contention. Emad argued that God only loves those who are repentant and godly. Allah loves faithful law-keepers; Allah does not love the wicked. I replied that God loves the wicked precisely because "God is love" (1 John 4:8). Therefore, God has purposed to be gracious to us in the person and work of his Son. Emad recoiled at the notion that God is love. Allah

---

[1] This debate, "A Friendly Debate: Session 1 'Who is God?'" with Emad Meerza, former emir of Islam for Kern County, California, took place February 24, 2020, at Laurelglen Bible Church and is accessible at https://vimeo.com/390870064.

does love. But Allah does not love the undeserving sinner. Thus, Allah is not love.

Our understanding of God informs everything else we believe and proclaim about our faith. Proclaiming the true God is central to the missionary task of making disciples. The apostles consistently began their evangelistic messages by teaching about who God is.[2] They believed it was necessary to correct false understandings of God prior to announcing the nature and state of man, our need for forgiveness, and God's provision in the gospel of Jesus Christ. Thus, we believe it is imperative that we begin with understanding God if we hope to be faithful to the Great Commission given by Christ to his church.

Without God blazing at the center, missions becomes a hollow, man-centered activity for the general social good. This kind of missions work does not save men from eternal condemnation. It is not motivated by worship of God, nor does it lead to the worship of God. It is a secular, humanitarian effort akin to the Peace Corps or a United Nations program. But true Christian missions is radically God-centered—springing from, and leading to, worship of our triune Lord.

Christian missions is about making our triune Lord known to those who have suppressed the truth in unrighteousness, and who are justly condemned to eternal perdition, so they might be reconciled and restored to him (Rom 1:8–32; see also 3:9–26). Thus, in the ordinary course, the positive impact of our missionary efforts will never truly exceed our depth of understanding of the doctrine of God and his saving work. While God may, as some say, draw a straight line with a crooked stick—that is, he may use us despite our own ill motives or lack of preparation—we are responsible to show ourselves workmen approved (2 Tim 2:15). We cannot expect to hit the mark in our missionary efforts unless we are aiming at the right target. Jesus understood this well. In fact, his commission to the church is a command to make disciples of our triune Lord: "And Jesus came and said to them, 'All authority in heaven and on earth has been given to me. Go therefore and make disciples of all nations, baptizing them in the name of the

---

2 See chapter 6 for more.

Father and of the Son and of the Holy Spirit, teaching them to observe all that I have commanded you. And behold, I am with you always, to the end of the age'" (Matt 28:18–20).

Jesus grounded the Great Commission in the authority that has been given to him. As the Christ, he has been given that authority by his Father (Ps 2:7–9; Dan 7:13–14; John 17:1–5). Jesus then provided the central thrust of his command, telling the apostles to go and make disciples of all nations.[3] What is the means of making disciples among all nations? Jesus employed two words that tell us the means: "baptizing" and "teaching."[4] The church is to go and make disciples of all nations by the means of baptizing them into the name of the Father and of the Son and of the Holy Spirit by teaching them to obey all that Jesus commanded. Jesus is Lord and is to be obeyed and worshiped as such (Matt 28:17–20). Finally, he promised the power for accomplishing the Great Commission. Jesus will be with them always, by the Holy Spirit (John 14:16–17, see also v. 23), to the end of the age (Matt 28:20).

The Great Commission is thoroughly Trinitarian. We are sent and empowered by our triune Lord to make disciples of our triune Lord. When disciples are made, they are identified in baptism with the name of the Father and of the Son and of the Holy Spirit. Baptism is a naming ceremony in which new disciples take the singular name of our triune Lord upon them. The name is singular as the LORD our God is one (Deut 6:4). The singular name is that of the Father and of the Son and of the Holy Spirit, as the persons are three—one God in three persons.[5] This is the God of the Bible, the God who has created and redeemed us, the God we worship. The church confesses the mystery

---

3 We take the participle "go" as one that attends the circumstance of the primary imperatival verb "make disciples" and thus is part of the command. See Daniel B. Wallace, *Greek Grammar beyond the Basics: An Exegetical Syntax of the New Testament* (Grand Rapids: Zondervan, 1996), 640. As to the definition of "nations," see chapter 7.

4 "Baptizing" and "teaching" are both participles of means explaining how disciples are to be made.

5 The Greek grammar of this Trinitarian formula has an article before each person, distinguishing them as three persons in the one name.

of the Trinity because it was taught by our Lord Jesus. This was well understood in church history. The fourth-century church father Gregory of Nazianzus, in his "Oratio on Baptism," wrote in AD 381, "No sooner do I conceive of the One than I am illumined by the Splendor of the Three; no sooner do I distinguish Them than I am carried back to the One. When I think of any One of the Three I think of Him as the Whole, and my eyes are filled, and the greater part of what I am thinking of escapes me."[6]

The identity of our triune Lord is central to the task of missions. We have received the triune name as our family name in baptism, and we are calling others to be born again and baptized into this same family. Worshiping and proclaiming the true God is not an exercise in academic theology. Rather, the "doctrine of the Trinity is the foundation of all our communion with God, and comfortable dependence on Him."[7] Who God is stands as the most foundational article of our faith.

We cannot fulfill the Great Commission if we do not make disciples of the true God. Thus, our goal in the next three chapters is to cover each person in the Trinity and how missions is properly understood in light of who God is and what he is doing. We begin with the person of the Father. We will look first at the *person* of the Father and then the *work* of the Father.

THE PERSON OF THE FATHER

Who is the Father? What does the Bible tell us about him? We are told that he is the one God, from whom are all things and for whom we exist (1 Cor 8:6). He is the Creator. In him we live and move and have our being (Acts 17:28). He is the Sustainer. He is the God who created us as image-bearers that we might multiply and reflect his image throughout the earth (Gen 1:26–28). He is the Sovereign over all

---

[6] Gregory Nazianzen, "Select Orations of Saint Gregory Nazianzen," in *S. Cyril of Jerusalem, S. Gregory Nazianzen*, ed. Philip Schaff and Henry Wace, trans. Charles Gordon Browne and James Edward Swallow, *A Select Library of the Nicene and Post-Nicene Fathers of the Christian Church*, Second Series (New York: Christian Literature Company, 1894), 7:375.

[7] 2LCF 2.3.

(Acts 4:24–28). God does all his holy will upon the earth. He is the God whom we are to trust, obey, and worship (Deut 6:4–9).

Perhaps the most well-known description of God the Father is provided by the Lord Jesus in John 3:16: "For God so loved the world, that he gave his only Son, that whoever believes in him should not perish but have eternal life." The Father is the God who *so loved the world* that he gave his only Son. This is a phrase we often hear and seldom spend enough time meditating on. It is the love of the Father that is the fountain of his decree to send the Son into the world to save us. The Father, out of the overflow of his love for the world, gave his only begotten Son.

In meditating on this glorious truth, two questions must be considered. First, who is "the world"? Second, why does God love the world? The Greek word translated "world" (*kosmos*) can be a reference to the *physical planet*, as we see in the first use of "world" in John 3:17. The Greek word can also be used to refer to the *people* in the world, as it must in John 3:16. People believe. People perish for sin. People receive eternal life. People are saved. This statement may have startled the Jewish followers of Jesus. The Father's love is set upon fallen humanity. His love is not limited by ethnic distinctions. God so loved Jews, Samaritans, and Gentiles. God so loved the peoples from every tribe, tongue, and nation. God has sent his Son to be the Savior of the world, not just of ethnic Jews (John 4:42).

But why does God love the world? Why does the Father love sinful, perishing people who are condemned already (John 3:17–21)? The Bible is replete with references to God's love for sinners. It is God who showed his love for us in that while we were still sinners, Christ died for us (Rom 5:8). The Father gave his Son for us *because* he loves us, not *so that* he might love us. Why? What is the source of the Father's love for sinners? His own being and character. God is love—eternally and unchangeably love (1 John 4:8; 4:16).

God did not become loving when he created. God *is* love (1 John 4:16). God was not wooed into loving us by something admirable and beautiful in us. God's love is not something he appended to himself when he gazed upon his creature. God is love. God did not need to create an object for his love. God is eternally in a loving fellowship of the Father, the Son, and the Holy Spirit. God did not fall in love with us because of our love for him. He loved us first (1 John 4:10). The sixteenth-century Protestant Reformer Martin Luther rightly said, "The love of God does not find, but creates, that which is pleasing to it."[8] We did not deserve God's love. We deserved his just wrath for our sin. We are rebellious and hell-bound sinners who have violated the law of God (Eph 2:1–3), sinners who denied God and turned to worship the creation rather than the Creator (Rom 1:18–31; 3:9–20). "But God, being rich in mercy, because of the great love with which he loved us, even when we were dead in our trespasses, made us alive together with Christ—by grace you have been saved" (Eph 2:4–5).

THE WORK OF THE FATHER

The Father's love for us is the fountain from which his work for us flows. God created and redeems us out of the overflow of his love. For God so loved the world that *he gave* his only Son. Fundamental to the Father's love for us is self-giving. The Father loved, and so he *gave*. How was the love of the Father made manifest among us? He *sent* his only Son into the world to be the wrath-bearer for our sins (1 John 4:9–10). The Father loved us, so the Father *gave* or *sent* his only begotten Son. He gave his Son that we might not perish but have eternal life. Our just condemnation was death, but we received eternal life in Christ as a gift from God (Rom 6:23). We did nothing to merit this gracious gift. It is a gift that is all of grace, given in love.

God decreed to give us this gracious gift before we ever believed. He set his love upon us in the giving of this gift while we were still sinners. He chose to be gracious to us before we were ever born. The Father lovingly decreed to bless us with this grace before the foundation of the world (Eph 1:3–6). The Father was not motivated to do this because of some foreseen good in us. The Westminster Assembly

---

8 Martin Luther, *Heidelberg Disputation* 28 (1518).

confessed the following: "Those of mankind that are predestinated unto life, God, before the foundation of the world was laid, according to his eternal and immutable purpose, and the secret counsel and good pleasure of his will, hath chosen, in Christ, unto everlasting glory, out of his mere free grace and love, without any foresight of faith, or good works, or perseverance in either of them, or any other thing in the creature, as conditions, or causes moving him thereunto; and all to the praise of his glorious grace."[9]

God is immutably loving, and his love is not made hot or cold based on our relative goodness. God is love because he is who he is. John Calvin stated this well:

> If you ask why the world has been created, why we have been placed in it to rule over the earth, why we are preserved in life to enjoy innumerable blessings, why we are endued with light and understanding, no other reason can be given except the free love of God. . . . It was not only an immeasurable love that God did not spare his own Son, that by his death he might restore us to life; it was also the most marvelous goodness, which should fill our minds with the greatest wonder and amazement. *Christ, then, is so illustrious and remarkable a proof of divine love toward us that whenever we look at him, he fully confirms the truth that God is love.*[10]

APPLICATION

Knowing the Father eternally decreed our salvation and sent his Son out of the overflow of his love for sinners like us necessarily affects our missionary practice. We cannot preach the gospel if we fail to understand that the Father loves justly condemned sinners. He first loved us. In Christ, love came down to save us. The Father was not provoked to send his Son by essentially good people seeking to worship him. There are no noble savages. No one is righteous. No, not one. "No one seeks for God" (Rom 3:9–11). Christianity is not the story of mankind seeking the true God. It is the story of God seeking to save rebellious

---

9 WCF 3.5, emphasis added. See also 2LCF 3.5.
10 John Calvin and Matthew Henry, *1, 2, & 3 John*, Crossway Classic Commentaries (Wheaton, IL: Crossway, 1998), 79, emphasis added.

sinners fleeing his presence. Christ was sent by the Father to seek and save the lost. He sends us in the Great Commission to do the same.

Although not all the unreached peoples of the world are Muslim, it is helpful to draw contrast with Islam here in particular. The god of Islam, Allah, is not love. He has love, but he is not love. He does not love wicked creatures. He loves only the repentant and virtuous. In other words, his love is aroused by the creature. The God of Christianity is love. The Father sent and gave his Son out of the overflow of his love. The Father does not love us because of Jesus. The Father loves us; therefore, he sent Jesus. If we fail to understand who the Father is, we will fail to understand the good news of the gospel message.

The saving love of the Father cannot be preached, nor can disciples of the Son be made, apart from proclaiming the triunity of God and baptizing in the triune name. If we deny that God is three in one, then we deny that God is eternally Father and that Jesus is eternally Son. Islam denies this truth in Surah 112 of the Qur'an: "In the name of God, the Gracious, the Merciful. Say, 'He is God, the One. God, the Absolute. He begets not, nor was he begotten. And there is none comparable to him.'" Allah does not "beget." Thus, he is not eternally Father. God is not begotten. Thus, he is not eternally Son. Allah is a single-person god. He is not the triune God of creation, providence, and redemption. Allah is not the God who is progressively revealed in the prophets of the Old Testament and finally and fully revealed in the incarnation of the Son (Heb 1:1–2).

We cannot overestimate the impact of understanding the love of God, originating from the Father and expressed in Christ. For those inculcated in an Islamic worldview, with which we have dealt only briefly in this chapter, the realization of the love of God is revolutionary. Consider this testimony ascribed to a Ghanaian man named Komna, a former muezzin (a Muslim who shouts the call to prayer from atop the minaret of a *masjid*, or mosque) who converted from Islam to the Christian faith: "I understood that Jesus alone could answer my question about eternal security. . . . I decided to trust Christ, and from that moment I felt that I was no longer the same person. Truly, I felt like a huge burden had been lifted. An indescribable joy came over me, as if I had discovered a treasure. This was actually the case because I had become a co-heir with Jesus. Glory to God!"[11] The God of the Bible alone offers—and evidences—the sort of unconditional love that can absolve the guilty human conscience, offer assurance of one's eternal destiny, and accomplish peace with God.

All our missionary efforts are to be informed by the love of God. The love of Christ compels us to make him known (2 Cor 5:14). God's love is self-giving, and our love is to imitate his. His love is not based on the merit in the object he loves but on the virtue of love in the Giver. In turn, we are to love in such a manner that we sacrifice everything for others, even enemies (Eph 5:1–2; see also Matt 5:43–48). But this self-giving love does not arise from our fallen hearts; it is the fruit of the Holy Spirit (Gal 5:22).

As God's love has descended from heaven to earth in the person of the Son, so the love of God in us compels us to cross land and sea to proclaim the good news in Christ Jesus. The love of the Father is not set peculiarly on one ethnic group, language, or geographical location; it is set on his people in every tribe, tongue, and nation. The glorious good news that the Father loves sinners like us and gave his Son to save us is the ground of our assurance of provision, the basis for our consolation in persecution and suffering, and the cause for our partnership with missionaries sent forth by the church (Matt 6:26–33; Rom 8:28–39; 3 John 5–8).

---

11 Hannah Strayer, "How One African Went from Shouting the Muslim Call to Prayer to Sharing the Call of Christ," *ABWE Blog*, ABWE International, January 15, 2020, https://www.abwe.org/blog/how-one-african-went-shouting-muslim-call-prayer-sharing-call-christ.

STUDY QUESTIONS

1. Why is it necessary to begin with God whenever we preach the gospel? How does beginning with God remind us of the motive and object of our mission?

2. In what ways do you think the average Westerner is confused about the gospel because of his confusion about who God is?

3. How do you think Islam's understanding of a monistic (single-person) God who is not "love" would confuse Muslim hearers of the gospel if you did not correct their understanding of God?

4. How do you think Buddhist pantheism (believing all is God) would confuse a Buddhist hearer of the gospel if you did not correct their understanding of God?

5. How do you think animistic and spiritist hearers of the gospel would be confused if you did not correct their understanding of God?

6. Would it be irresponsible to proclaim the gospel without knowing what people hear when we speak about God? What does our responsibility to begin with God suggest about the level at which we must know language and culture to clearly communicate the gospel? What does this reality suggest about how long it would take to learn a culture and language, proclaim the gospel to that people, and ground a church on these doctrinal truths in their language and culture?

7. How does the love of Christ compel us to do the hard work of learning language and culture, risking comfort and safety, to make the gospel clear to unreached peoples? How does the love of God in Christ compel our churches to share in this missionary work (3 John 5–8)?

3

THE SON'S MISSION TO SAVE ALL NATIONS

All authority in heaven and on earth has been given to me.
Matthew 28:18

I (Alex) once heard of a missionary in India who visited a Hindu family who had a collection of small idols displayed on their mantle. When the family heard about Jesus, they simply added a small portrait of Jesus to their collection—an unsurprising example of *syncretism*, or mixing Christianity with pagan religion. In this case, Jesus was treated as another one of Hinduism's countless gods. But when the missionary returned some months later, the image of Jesus alone now occupied the prime location over the hearth. Why? In the time between the missionary's visits, a Hindu priest had also visited the home. Upon seeing the mantle, he had remarked, "Why are they all together? *This* one" indicating Jesus, "is the *God of gods.*" His comment was the seed that began to change the family's perspective.

Missions-minded Christians should not be surprised at the reminder that the Lord Jesus Christ stands utterly apart from all rival gods. But there is less consensus—even in the missions community—about what exactly Christ has *done*. Why did Christ die and rise? One growing school in missiology argues that a gospel emphasizing legal remission of sins before God the Judge is insufficient for Majority World hearers, whose cultures place more weight on the dynamics of honor and shame or fear and power than on guilt and innocence.[1] One writer attributes "emphasis on the legal aspects of salvation" to a "Western gospel" and maintains that the "introspective guilt" of men like Augustine of Hippo and Martin Luther led to a theology accommodated to an "individualistic, rationalistic and guilt-based" culture.[2] Elsewhere, the writer claims (anachronistically) that the Protestant Reformers' "Enlightenment worldview" led them to substitute cultural categories such as honor and shame with "socio-moral logic (i.e., punitive justice, penal substitution)" with regard to the work of Christ.[3]

Is Christ a substitute for sinners, a savior from shame, a demon-slaying hero for the powerless, or some combination of all three? The gospel is nothing if not multifaceted, yet modern explanations of the gospel framed through these differing cultural paradigms range from well-intentioned and biblical to questionable and sinister. The difference between worshiping a Jesus who sits among the other "deities" on one's shelf and a Jesus who sits enthroned as Lord of lords is the difference between eternal death and eternal life. In his commission to the church, Jesus reminds us that he possesses "all authority in heaven and on earth" (Matt 28:18). If we get Jesus wrong, nothing else we do in missions, evangelism, or church planting matters.

We have seen so far that because God has spoken sufficiently and inerrantly in his Word, Scripture gives us not only our message but also our methods for ministry. We've also seen that the missionary heart of God stems from his triune nature, the relationships within the Godhead spilling out into love for the world, and that God the Father is

---

[1] Some of the better-known missiological texts advocating this approach include Roland Muller, *Honor and Shame: Unlocking the Door* (Bloomington, IN: Xlibris Corporation, 2001); Jackson Wu, *Reading Romans with Eastern Eyes: Honor and Shame in Paul's Message and Mission* (United Kingdom: InterVarsity Press, 2019), and Jayson Georges, *The 3D Gospel: Ministry in Guilt, Shame, and Fear Cultures* (Timē Press, 2014).

[2] Jayson Georges and Mark D. Baker, *Ministering in Honor-Shame Cultures: Biblical Foundations and Practical Essentials* (Downers Grove: IVP Academic, 2016), 22.

[3] Jayson Georges, "Improving Anselm's Theory of the Atonement," Honor-Shame, updated April 3, 2017, http://honorshame.com/improving-anselms-atonement-theory.

the fountainhead of love from which God's mission to the world flows. Naturally, we now turn our attention to the Son of God.

PSALM 2 AND THE PERSON AND WORK OF CHRIST

To know Jesus and apply our knowledge of him to the missionary endeavor, we must consider him in at least two respects: his *person* and his *work*. Conveniently, Psalm 2 is one passage in which both aspects of the Son are vividly and profoundly set forth.

Background

Psalm 2 is regarded as an *enthronement* psalm. In its original context, this psalm speaks of the glory of King David and his heirs ruling righteously over the people of God. But these types of psalms also make audacious statements that cannot be said of any mere fallen man. They point away from the original, imperfect David to the true and better Son of David who was one day to rule God's people and save them from their enemies. The psalmists, including David himself, were looking forward to the full realization of Yahweh's covenant promise to David: "When your days are fulfilled and you lie down with your fathers, I will raise up your offspring after you, who shall come from your body, and I will establish his kingdom. He shall build a house for my name, and I will establish the throne of his kingdom forever" (2 Sam 7:12–13).

Psalm 2 is also a *missionary* psalm. When the twelve apostles were first preaching the gospel and faced with persecution, they turned to this passage for comfort (see Acts 4:23–31). They knew it spoke of the present power of the Jesus they had just seen crucified and raised. So, released from prison and warned to stay silent, Peter wove the words of this psalm into his prayer, and "when they had prayed, the place in which they were gathered together was shaken, and they were all filled with the Holy Spirit and continued to speak the word of God with boldness" (v. 31). It is our prayer that through studying this psalm, we too might receive such power for mission.

Seething Sinners, Suffering Servant

Psalm 2 begins, "Why do the nations rage and the peoples plot in vain? The kings of the earth set themselves, and the rulers take counsel together, against the Lord and against his Anointed, saying, 'Let us burst their bonds apart and cast away their cords from us'" (vv. 1–3). The stage is set, and it is full of bad actors. David's life was full of enemies who sought to do him harm, but this only foreshadowed the reproach endured by Jesus. Peter connects the raging and plotting of the nations, rulers, and kings with the conspiracy of Herod, Pontius Pilate, and the other rulers to crucify Jesus (Acts 4:27).

This brings us to the very reason for which the divine Son, on the basis of his eternal covenant with the Father to redeem a people for God, became incarnate: *there is no such thing as neutrality* before a holy God. Since Adam fell into sin and plunged humanity into rebellion, each human being begins life at war with his Creator (Ps 51:5; Rom 5:12). Sinful rebels like Herod and Pilate are stand-ins for mankind itself in its every seething attempt to cast off the rule of God: "None is righteous, no, not one; no one understands; no one seeks for God" (Rom 3:10–11; see also Ps 14:1–3). This places humanity under the wrath of God, who in his holiness cannot endure the sight of sin in his presence (Hab 1:13).

We are also reminded of the identity of God the Son. Note that the hostility of sinners is toward not just a generic deity but against the triune God himself—against Israel's God and his "Anointed"—his Christ. The Father and the Son cannot be separated; if men reject one, they necessarily reject both (1 John 2:23). The Son is in unbreakable union with the Father (John 10:30) and represents him perfectly as the Word (John 1:1; Heb 1:3). This Word, eternally one with God in being and yet distinct from the Father and Spirit in person, became flesh (John 1:14), assuming a human nature (Phil 2:7), born of the virgin Mary under God's moral law (Gal 4:4), fully like us yet without sin (Heb 4:15). The Chalcedonian Definition teaches that the Lord Jesus Christ is "truly God and truly man, of a reasonable soul and body; consubstantial with us according to the manhood . . . to be acknowledged in two natures, inconfusedly, unchangeably, indivisibly, inseparably... in one Person and one Subsistence, not parted or divided into two persons, but one and the same Son, and only begotten, God the Word, the Lord Jesus Christ."[4]

Because we confess that the Lord Jesus Christ, the incarnate Son of God, is both one unified person and indivisible from the Father and the Spirit according to his divine nature, then since the unreached are naturally hostile to God (Rom 8:7), they are also naturally hostile to Jesus. To reject any person in the triune God is to reject all three divine persons. Psalm 2 reflects the fact that mankind's rebellion against the Creator God extends to rebellion against Christ himself.

Yet this hostile rebellion—the raging of the nations against God and Christ—is not accidental but planned. Christ came to die on purpose. All this was according to "the definite plan and foreknowledge of God" (Acts 2:23). Because God must uphold justice and punish sin, and because God had decreed to save a special people as the object of his love, it was necessary that an atoning sacrifice be made. Before he ruled as the conquering King of Psalm 2, Jesus came as the suffering Servant of Isaiah 53. The Father poured out his wrath on Christ on the cross in our place in a penal, substitutionary atonement so that he could forgive sinners justly while satisfying the demands of divine justice. Jesus was "a propitiation by his blood, to be received by faith... to show [God's] righteousness at the present time, so that he might be just and the justifier of the one who has faith in Jesus" (Rom 3:25–26). Our guilt was placed on Christ, and his perfect obedience to the law of God is imputed to us (2 Cor 5:21).[5]

---

4 The Definition of the Council of Chalcedon (AD 451).
5 Because Christ's death actually accomplishes salvation to be applied by the Spirit and does not merely make men potentially savable in such a way as to leave them to finish the process, the atonement applies necessarily to the particular, elect people of God and not to every individual (including those who will persist in unbelief and suffer damnation) as is often assumed. This doctrine of particular redemption has been a perennial source of misunderstanding among Protestants, but it is worth noting here that the limited scope of the atonement reinforces, rather than opposes, the missionary call. For more, see Alex Kocman, "3 Reasons Definite Atonement is Basic to Biblical Missions," Founders Ministries, January 21, 2019, https://founders.org/2019/01/21/3-reasons-definite-atonement-is-basic-to-biblical-missions.

The concept of penal, substitutionary atonement, far from being a Western formulation of the gospel, *is* pure gospel. It comes not from Greco-Roman legal tradition but grows from the soil of the Old Testament sacrificial system—which God embedded, interestingly, in an ancient *Near Eastern* culture (not Western) to prepare the world to make sense of the Messiah. Consider, for instance, the ceremony surrounding the Day of Atonement (Leviticus 16), in which the high priest confessed transgression on behalf of the people and laid his hands on the sacrificial animal, symbolically transferring the nation's guilt to it. In turn, the prophet predicted of Christ, "But he was pierced for our transgressions; he was crushed for our iniquities; upon him was the chastisement that brought us peace, and with his wounds we are healed" (Isa 53:5). It is true that the gospel has rich implications for cultures steeped in the dynamics of honor and shame associated with communalism or the fear and power latent in animistic contexts. But these implications flow from Christ's having propitiated and expiated our guilt. It is because we are forgiven and declared righteous in Christ that we can be freed from shame and fear (see Heb 4:14–16; 10:19–22). Because we are justified, we belong to the society of the redeemed, a community in which there is no shame (Rom 10:9–13). Because we are justified, the evil spirits in the world can no longer wield our guilt against us, and Satan the accuser and his demonic horde have lost any right over us (Col 2:14–15; John 12:31). These are not alternative emphases to penal substitution but are necessary outgrowths of the doctrine. In sum, "Christ Jesus came into the world to save sinners" (1 Tim 1:15).

But the story of Psalm 2 does not stop at the cross.

Divine Comedy

In the next verses, God responds to man's rebellion: "He who sits in the heavens laughs; the Lord holds them in derision. Then he will speak to them in his wrath, and terrify them in his fury, saying, 'As for me, I have set my King on Zion, my holy hill'" (vv. 4–6). If verses 1–3 allude to the Messiah's crucifixion, what does it mean that God laughs (v. 4) and establishes his King on his "holy hill" (v. 6)? First, this victorious coronation of Christ begins when, on the third day after his death, Christ rose. Death could not hold him (Acts 2:24). His resurrection attests to the sufficient, sacrificial nature of his death. His work on the cross was finished and received by God. Moreover, to accomplish full salvation for his people, it was not enough that he simply take their place in death, but he also needed to emerge triumphant to bring them back into the presence of the living God. He was raised for our justification (Rom 4:25). And if he were not raised, then we are still in our sins (1 Cor 15:17). His resurrection is the down payment on the resurrection of our physical bodies in sinless glory at the last day (John 11:25; Rom 5:17; 1 Cor 15:22–23). Because he lives, we will live (John 14:19).

But the resurrection of Christ is even more than a receipt for a transaction. Consider the concept of *comedy*. The term today generally refers to film or literature designed to elicit laughter. In classical Greco-Roman culture, a comedy was a story of heroic triumph that culminated in a wedding celebration. We might describe the resurrection and victory of Christ as a true "comedy" in both respects, though our text obviously predates the later classical literary genre. In Psalm 2:4–6, God bellows a hearty laugh at the futility of human rebellion and raises his Son from the dead to reign as King of kings, defeat Satan, and be united to his bride, the church (Acts 2:36; Eph 5:25–27; 1 John 3:8; Rev 1:5). In fact, the whole biblical story is a comedy, from Jesus's victory over Eden's serpent (Gen 3:15) to his marriage to his redeemed people (Rev 19:7–9). In short, to borrow a phrase used by others, Jesus killed the dragon and got the girl. And this victory has abiding implications for the church's task. As we will see, the installation of Christ as King continues beyond the resurrection.

Risen Now to Reign

When I was a youth pastor, I was fond of asking our students, "Where is Jesus right now?" On one such occasion, I was met by a handful of middle school boys with quizzical stares until finally a few brave souls chimed in: "He's everywhere." "He's in our hearts." One of the boys piped up, "He's watching over the dinosaurs." Unfortunately, I suspect a group of adults in the average evangelical church would not poll much better. We stop at the resurrection and forget the *ascension* of Christ and his present *session* in heaven—God's "holy hill." Yet all Christians are to confess that Jesus ascended bodily into heaven and sat down to rule at the right hand of the Father (Acts 1:9; 2:33). Enthroned over the cosmos, Jesus Christ is interceding on behalf of his people (Rom 8:34) and putting all his enemies under his feet (Ps 110:1; 1 Cor 15:24–27) through his providence and the gospel witness of the church (Matt 28:18–19; Rom 5:10; 2 Cor 10:4–6; Rev 12:11).

The reality of Christ's present rule over his kingdom is the basis of our mission to the nations. Psalm 2 continues: "I will tell of the decree: The LORD said to me, 'You are my Son; today I have begotten you. Ask of me, and I will make the nations your heritage, and the ends of the earth your possession. You shall break them with a rod of iron and dash them in pieces like a potter's vessel'" (vv. 7–9).

In its original historic context, this section of the psalm again speaks in exalted language of the intimate relationship between David, his dynasty, and Israel's God. Yet the strong paternal language points far beyond David to the divine Son himself. So, when did this conversation between God the Father and the Son occur? Was it at Christ's baptism, when he heard, "You are my beloved Son; with you I am well pleased" from heaven (Luke 3:22)? Was it on the Mount of Transfiguration when the announcement was repeated (Matt 17:5)? In fact, God's fatherly approval of the Son cannot be constrained to a single moment of time. The Father loves the Son eternally. The Son has always been equal in power to the Father in the Godhead. The idea that Jesus "became" God's Son as a reward for his obedience at some point in his human lifetime is an ancient heresy called *adoptionism*, condemned univocally by the church at least since the First Council of Nicaea in AD 325. When the Father tells the Son "today I have begotten you," Scripture provides a glimpse into the timeless relationships inside the Godhead—where "today" is never-ending, and each divine person is without temporal beginning or end. The Son always was, is, and will be the image and radiance of the Father and is thus the only way for us to know God (Heb 1:1–2).

Nevertheless, the Son had covenanted with the Father in eternity "past" (2 Tim 1:9; Titus 1:2) to accomplish redemption for God's people and receive a kingdom *in human history*: "The Father loves the Son and has given all things into his hand" (John 3:35). When the Son took on human form, this rise into his kingdom had to be experienced in time and space. Psalm 110, the Old Testament text most frequently cited by the New Testament writers, connects the incarnate Son's authority with his ascension to the right hand of God:

> The LORD says to my Lord:
> "Sit at my right hand
> until I make your enemies your footstool."
> The Lord sends forth from Zion
> your mighty scepter.
> Rule in the midst of your enemies! (vv. 1–2)

The New Testament attests that Christ's ascension marks his installation as King. The Son already ruled the universe according to his divine nature, but it was necessary that according to his human nature he might save all the nations and spread his rule throughout the world following his resurrection. This is because the first representative of humanity had royally failed as God's image-bearing vice-regent. Christ had to accomplish what Adam did not. During his earthly ministry, Jesus anticipated that upon his ascension he would receive authority over his kingdom, invoking Daniel's prophetic vision of the Son of Man in the throne room of heaven:

> "I saw in the night visions,
> and behold, with the clouds of heaven
> there came one like a son of man,
> and he came to the Ancient of Days
> and was presented before him.

> And to him was given dominion
> and glory and a kingdom,
> that all peoples, nations, and languages
> should serve him;
> his dominion is an everlasting dominion,
> which shall not pass away,
> and his kingdom one
> that shall not be destroyed." (Daniel 7:13–14)

Though we often associate this scene with the consummate return of Christ at the end of history, Jesus connected it with the events surrounding his redemptive work in the first century. Jesus warned his interrogators in his trial that they would "see" the Son of Man seated and ruling "from now on" (Matt 26:64; see also Mark 14:62). Whereas Satan had offered him dominion over the nations upon condition of full surrender (Luke 4:5–7), Jesus secured his global kingdom by triumphing over Satan on the cross, casting him out of the heavenly places (John 12:31) and receiving authority from the Father.

This is why in Psalm 2:8, upon Christ's exaltation, God the Father tells the royal Son, "Ask of me, and I will make the nations your heritage, and the ends of the earth your possession." Consider the sheer weight of this offer! Christ was only to ask, and the nations were to be his. Ought we to conclude anything other than that Christ accepted the offer? Christ, having accomplished what the first Adam failed to do on behalf of the human race (Rom 5:12–21), became the head of a new humanity and fulfilled the promise made to Abraham to bless all nations and families of the earth (Gen 12:3). It is no surprise, then, that when the time had arrived for Jesus to commission his apostles, he began the Great Commission by stating that *all authority in heaven and earth had been given to him.* Because he has this authority, the church is not only to engage in personal evangelism but to disciple the nations (Matt 28:19). And Jesus will continue to rule from heaven until the nations have been effectively discipled and all his elect have been saved (1 Cor 15:24–25; 2 Pet 3:9).

Perhaps, considering the apparent disarray of the world, we are tempted to think "King of kings and Lord of lords" is merely an honorific title and that Jesus wields little actual power over the course of history. Yet as Psalm 2 further unfolds, it leads us to a different conclusion.

Wisdom and Warning

The second psalm shifts its tone in the final stanzas, addressing the hostile, onlooking world:

> Now therefore, O kings, be wise;
>
> be warned, O rulers of the earth.
>
> Serve the LORD with fear,
>
> and rejoice with trembling.
>
> Kiss the Son,
>
> lest he be angry, and you perish in the way,
>
> for his wrath is quickly kindled.
>
> Blessed are all who take refuge in him. (vv. 10–12)

Jesus is not just King, in a pious sense, over some ethereal realm. His dominion challenges the existing anti-Christian power structures and principalities (v. 10). His rule results in the authoritative warning that all nations and peoples of the earth are to "wise up" and surrender to him and receive his terms of peace. Perhaps this is what Paul had in mind when he described his apostolic ministry as "*warning* everyone and teaching everyone with all *wisdom*, that we may present everyone mature in Christ" (Col 1:28, emphasis added). The gospel goes forth not only as a warm invitation to experience salvation but also as a solemn counsel to flee the wrath of God.

The good news of Jesus's death, resurrection, ascension, and rule demands a response. That response is repentance and faith. Kings and commoners alike must "kiss the Son" (v. 12)—pay homage to him, coming humbly to him with the honor of faith (see John 5:23). Those who do not respond in the humility of faith remain under God's judgment as well as the wrath of Christ himself (Rev 6:16). But for those who come to Christ, he stands to receive them as a refuge from wrath: "Whoever comes to me I will never cast out" (John 6:37). This is the good news of salvation, but it is a two-edged sword; the Christian message offers grace freely to all yet is a profoundly *exclusive* faith. Jesus Christ is the *only* way to God (John 14:6). The idea of a "noble savage" entitled to eternal life by virtue of his inherent goodness apart from Christ makes no sense in light of the radical payment offered at the cross, which was futile if all roads lead to heaven. Men and women of all nations must kiss the Son.

Application

In a postmodern age of emotionality, private spirituality, and radical subjectivity, there is no surer way to make cultural enemies than to proselytize. What gives us the right to tell sincere followers of other religions their way is wrong and ours is right? Christ's lordship over all the peoples of earth gives us this right. The Great Commission is Christ's sending of his people to secure the faith and obedience of the nations that are already his.

Psalm 2 bears four important applications for the missionary task. First, we must engage the lost peoples of the world knowing that there is no neutrality; every human being is born in a state of hostile rebellion to God. Second, we are to proclaim Christ's crucifixion and exaltation to bring the kingdom of God to sinners. Third, the nations now belong to the Son, and his authority gives us the audacity to go. And fourth, we call the world to repent and believe—to fearfully, joyfully kiss the Son—finding refuge from his wrath through the cross.

The authoritative proclamation of the person and work of the Son is the heart and soul of the missionary enterprise. This is why William Carey, recognized as the father of modern missions, and his compatriots in Serampore, India, agreed together:

> In preaching to the heathen, we must keep to the example of Paul, and make the great subject of our preaching, Christ the Crucified. It would be very easy for a missionary to preach nothing but truths,

and that for many years together, without any well-grounded hope of becoming useful to one soul. The doctrine of Christ's expiatory death and all sufficient merits has been, and must ever remain, the grand means of conversion. This doctrine, and others immediately connected with it, have constantly nourished and sanctified the church. Oh that these glorious truths may ever be the joy and strength of our own souls, and then they will not fail to become the matter of our conversation to others.[6]

The Son of God has died, risen, and rules. His cross redeems sinners from the guilt of sin, and this message is immediately relevant to all nations and cultures. His mission to disciple the nations has been determined and will be fully accomplished in history. We simply share the privilege of being used by him through our proclamation of Christ and him crucified. This is what the missionary task is about.

STUDY QUESTIONS

1. Who is God the Son? Is he equal to God, less than God, separate from God, or a mere part of God? How does the divinity of the Son affect the way we talk about Jesus to individuals from other cultures?

2. Why did Christ have to die? What does this tell us about the spiritual state of the world's peoples? What did his death accomplish?

3. Is it necessary to speak about Christ's work in categories relating to guilt, punishment, and forgiveness in cross-cultural settings? Why or why not?

4. How does Christ's removal of our legal, forensic guilt before God address the problems of shame experienced in a

---

[6] "The Bond of the Missionary Brotherhood of Serampore, 1805," article 5 in George Smith, *The Life of William Carey, D.D., Shoemaker and Missionary* (Edinburgh: R. & R. Clark, 1885), 445. This document is more commonly known as the *Serampore Form of Agreement* and is referenced henceforth in this volume by article number and using the latter name.

collectivist society? If Christ's death were not penal and substitutionary, do the same applications still apply?

5. How does Christ's removal of our legal, forensic guilt before God address the problems of fear experienced in a power-driving, spiritist/animist society? If Christ's death were not penal and substitutionary, do the same applications still apply?

6. Why did Christ also need to rise from the dead? What is he doing now?

7. What are the implications of Christ's present activity for missionary boldness? What direction is history going under his providence?

8. How can an individual experience the benefits of Christ's work? How does this affect the missionary's message?

9. What do the psalmist and the apostle Paul mean by "warning" in the context of proclaiming the gospel?

10. Is there a way to be saved apart from Christ? Why or why not?

4

THE HOLY SPIRIT'S MISSION AS WITNESS TO CHRIST IN ALL NATIONS

And behold, I am sending the promise of my Father upon you. But stay in the city until you are clothed with power from on high.
Luke 24:49

"You are putting God in a box."

"There is a fresh wind of the Holy Spirit."

"The Spirit of God is doing new things that your old wineskins won't contain."

"We need to find where the Holy Spirit is at work and join him there."

"The Holy Spirit is doing something different in foreign nations."

These are all mantras regularly employed in discussions about missions methodologies. If you conclude that a particular method is unbiblical, there is no escape from the charge that you are in some way "quenching the Spirit." With the growing popularity of critical theories as lenses through which to interpret the arguments and actions of others, to question new missions methods can earn someone the charge of being a Pharisee, a naïve traditionalist, or a Western imperialist. Those who claim there is an *ordinary means*—a means that applies in every tribe, tongue, and nation—by which the Holy Spirit works are labeled as Eurocentric interpreters of Scripture.

The revivalism of modern evangelicalism is continually in search of new measures that will elicit the extraordinary work of the Holy Spirit and usher in an era of rapid multiplication of Christian disciples.[1] Once a missiologist has discovered a new method that gains rapid results, he instructs others to follow his formula to receive the blessing with which it has been endued by the Lord. We need to hitch our proverbial wagon to the engine of the Holy Spirit's present movement. We can recognize this work of the Holy Spirit on the basis of how many new disciples are being claimed.[2]

Protestants have historically argued that the Holy Spirit generally works through ordinary means. Those ordinary means are defined as preaching the Word and administering the ordinances of baptism and the Lord's Supper. The Westminster Confession of Faith summarized this: "The grace of faith, whereby the elect are enabled to believe to the saving of their souls, is the work of the Spirit of Christ in their hearts, and is ordinarily wrought by the ministry of the Word, by which also, and by the administration of the sacraments, and prayer, it is increased and strengthened."[3]

These ordinary means are placed in the hands of missionaries who patiently work to see God save his people and build up his church.

---

[1] "New measures" is the language of Charles Finney. For a deeper treatment of this topic outside the realm of cross-cultural missions, see Ian H. Murray, *Revival and Revivalism: The Making and Marring of American Evangelicalism 1750–1858* (Edinburgh: Banner of Truth, 1994). Many popular missiologists have moved away from the rapid multiplication of churches as "church planting movements" (CPM) have given way to "disciple making movements" (DMM).

[2] This standard has become particularly elusive in the most pervasive method of missions today: disciple-making movements. This method claims disciples of Jesus and the multiplication of churches without the necessity of outward conversion to Christianity or the historic marks of a church. See Chad Vegas, "A Brief Guide to DMM: Defining and Evaluating the Ideas Impacting Missions Today," Radius International, June 11, 2018, https://www.radiusinternational.org/a-brief-guide-to-dmm.

[3] WCF 14.1.

Many contemporary missions practitioners argue that to insist on these ordinary means is to impose "Western religion" and "ineffective strategies" in our missionary task—strategies that deny the extraordinary work of the Holy Spirit. Christ's church is not commanded to establish its methods on the basis of what God *can* do *extraordinarily* but rather what Christ has said his church *should* do *ordinarily*. God can do whatever he wants. This is not in question. What has God commanded his church to do? What is the *ordinary* work he has given to his church? This is the question.

To understand the ordinary means Christ has given his church in missions work, we must answer three key questions:

- Who is the Holy Spirit?
- What is his mission?
- How does he complete his mission?

It is vital that we remember that doctrine and practice walk together. Thus, we must know what the Bible teaches about the person and work of the Holy Spirit if we are to practice the Great Commission properly.

WHO IS THE HOLY SPIRIT?

The Holy Spirit is God. He is the third person of our triune Lord, of the same substance as the Father and the Son. The Father, the Son, and the Holy Spirit are three eternally distinct and co-equal persons in one divine essence. Each of the three persons subsists in the one God without any division of the essence of God. They do not each constitute a third of God's essence—God's essence is simple and undivided. There is one God in three persons. This is why Jesus commands us to be baptized in the *one* name of the Father and of the Son and of the Holy Spirit (Matt 28:19). Thus, we confess in the Second London Confession of Faith:

> In this divine and infinite Being there are three subsistences, the Father, the Word or Son, and Holy Spirit, of one substance, power,

and eternity, each having the whole divine essence, yet the essence undivided: the Father is of none, neither begotten nor proceeding; the Son is eternally begotten of the Father; the Holy Spirit proceeding from the Father and the Son; all infinite, without beginning, therefore but one God, who is not to be divided in nature and being, but distinguished by several peculiar relative properties and personal relations.[4]

As the confession rightly states, each person in God has distinct *relative properties* and *personal relations*. The Father is the unbegotten fountain of the Godhead. He is eternally related as the Father. The Son is the eternally begotten Son of the Father. He is eternally related as the Son. The Holy Spirit eternally proceeds from the Father and the Son. He is eternally related as the Holy Spirit. We have fathers and sons, so we have some idea of what is meant by the personal relations of *Father* and *Son*. We understand what it means to *beget* and to *be begotten*, even though we can't comprehend eternal begetting. But how do we understand the personal relation of the Holy Spirit? We have no analogues in our human relationships for him.

What we do know from Scripture is that the sending of the Holy Spirit to be in us is not a downgrade. Jesus spoke of the coming Holy Spirit as advantageous to the disciples: "Nevertheless, I tell you the truth: it is to your advantage that I go away, for if I do not go away, the Helper will not come to you. But if I go, I will send him to you" (John 16:7). Jesus going away and sending the Holy Spirit could be of no comparable advantage if the Holy Spirit were a creature. Thomas Aquinas, the thirteenth-century Dominican priest, rightly argued the following:

> [Some heretics] say that the Holy Spirit is a creature and the minister of the Father and the Son. But if this were true, the coming of the Holy Spirit would not have been a sufficient consolation to the apostles for Christ's leaving them. It would be like the departure of a king, where the substitution for him of one of his ministers would not be a sufficient consolation. Thus, because the Holy Spirit

---

4 2LCF 2.3; the WCF 2.3 employs the word "persons" rather than "subsistences." Both confessions attempt to communicate the same truth.

is equal to the Son, our Lord consoles them by promising that the Spirit will come.[5]

We know the Holy Spirit is sent by the Father and the Son (Luke 24:49; John 15:26). He eternally proceeds from them both. We affirm this scripturally revealed truth, but we are not sure how to understand it. As we attempt to apprehend the mystery of the Holy Trinity, we readily recognize that we come to the end of ourselves. We are finite creatures. We cannot comprehend the infinite Creator. One of the fourth-century Cappadocian fathers summed this up well: "Insofar as he [the Holy Spirit] proceeds from the Father, he is no creature; inasmuch as he is not begotten, he is no Son. . . . What then is Procession? Do you tell me what is the Unbegottenness of the Father, and I will explain to you the physiology of the Generation of the Son and the Procession of the Spirit, and we shall both of us be frenzy-stricken for prying into the mystery of God."[6]

The mystery of the Trinity, and our lack of resources for comprehending the procession of the Holy Spirit, is precisely why we must consider the work of the Holy Spirit among us. Like the Son, the Holy Spirit was sent on mission, and his mission among us gives us a better sense of his relation to the Father and the Son. The mission of the Son reveals Jesus to us. The same is true with the Holy Spirit.

WHAT IS THE MISSION OF THE HOLY SPIRIT?

The Son's mission is to redeem us (Eph 1:7–12).[7] The Holy Spirit's mission is to seal, or apply, the work of the Son to us (Eph 1:13–14). Jesus told his apostles to wait in Jerusalem until he sent the promise

---

5 Thomas Aquinas, *Commentary on the Gospel of John: Chapters 1–21*, trans. Fabian Larcher and James A. Weisheipl (Washington, DC: The Catholic University of America Press, 2010), 3:137.

6 Gregory Nazianzen, "Select Orations of Saint Gregory Nazianzen," in *S. Cyril of Jerusalem, S. Gregory Nazianzen*, ed. Philip Schaff and Henry Wace, trans. Charles Gordon Browne and James Edward Swallow, A Select Library of the Nicene and Post-Nicene Fathers of the Christian Church, Second Series (New York: Christian Literature Company, 1894), 7:320.

7 See chapter 3 for more on the work of the Son.

of the Father upon them, and they would be clothed with power from on high (Luke 24:49). He promised them he would baptize them with the Holy Spirit at Pentecost (Acts 1:4–5). For what end has the Father promised the Holy Spirit? Why is Jesus going to send the Holy Spirit and baptize his church with the Holy Spirit? What is the Holy Spirit coming to empower the apostles to do? The Holy Spirit would empower them to be the witnesses of Jesus in all the earth (Acts 1:8; Luke 24:47–48).

The Holy Spirit's mission is to be the witness of Christ (John 15:26–27). He witnesses to men's hearts in a manner the apostles never could (John 16:7–11). His mission is to make Jesus known and trusted among all his people (Luke 24:47–49; see also Acts 1:8). The Holy Spirit is the person who causes us to be born again in Christ (John 3:1–8; Titus 3:5). He gives us spiritual sight (1 Cor 2:10–14), bringing conversion to the lordship of Christ (1 Cor 12:3). He is the Comforter in that he brings us fellowship with the Father and the Son (John 14:16–17, 23; 2 Cor 13:14), unites us to the Son through faith (Rom 8:9–15), and thus adopts us as sons of the Father (Rom 8:15–17; see also Gal 4:4–6). He intercedes in our hearts and on our behalf (Rom 8:26–27).

The Holy Spirit encourages us as a seal and pledge of the resurrection life that is ours (Eph 1:13–14). He sheds the love of God abroad in our hearts (Rom 5:5). He actively works to illumine our minds and applies that truth to our hearts (Eph 1:16–18). He teaches Christ's people and causes them to remember him (John 16:12–15). He sanctifies us to be like Christ (2 Cor 3:18). The Holy Spirit testifies to us that we are children of God (Rom 8:15). In other words, the promises of God in Christ are brought to us personally and experientially by the Holy Spirit.

The Holy Spirit glorifies Christ (John 16:14–15), and so gives us a vision of something far greater than this world. He raises our minds to the things above, where Christ is seated, and we see him who is our life (Col 3:1–4). The Holy Spirit stirs our affections for Christ as our great treasure and unfading reward, and so we rejoice with joy inexpressible

(1 Pet 1:1–8). As the seventeenth-century English Puritan John Owen said, "And this is his work to the end of the world—to bring the promises of Christ to our minds and hearts, to give us the comfort of them, the joy and sweetness of them, much beyond that which the disciples found in them, when Christ in person spake them to them; their gracious influence being then restrained."[8]

This is the mission of the Holy Spirit. The Son was sent to purchase our redemption; the Holy Spirit was sent to apply the work of the Son to us.[9] The Holy Spirit gives us new birth into the new creation in Christ (2 Cor 5:17) and then empowers us to joyfully trumpet the good news of Christ's kingdom to every tribe, tongue, and nation for the salvation of men and the glory of God (Luke 24:47–49; see also Acts 1:8; Rom 1:5; 16:25–27).[10]

HOW DOES THE HOLY SPIRIT COMPLETE HIS MISSION?

The Holy Spirit ordinarily applies the work of Christ through the means he has given to the church: biblical preaching and ordinances. This *extraordinary work* of the Holy Spirit is accomplished through *ordinary means*. Jesus promised that the Holy Spirit would come to work through the ordinary preaching ministry of the apostles. Jesus told his disciples they would be his witnesses when the Holy Spirit came upon them. What would his witnesses do? They would proclaim the gospel. Jesus said to them, "Thus it is written, that the Christ should suffer and on the third day rise from the dead, and that repentance for the forgiveness of sins should be proclaimed in his name to all nations, beginning from Jerusalem" (Luke 24:46–47). This is precisely what we see the apostles doing throughout the book of Acts—the Holy Spirit

---

8 John Owen, *The Works of John Owen*, ed. William H. Goold (Edinburgh: Banner of Truth, 1965), 2:237.

9 The Heidelberg Catechism (1563), Q&A 53, says, "Q. What do you believe concerning the Holy Spirit? A. First, He is, together with the Father and the Son, true and eternal God. Second, He is also given to me, to make me by true faith share in Christ and all His benefits, to comfort me, and to remain with me forever."

10 For more on this important topic, see John Piper, *Let the Nations Be Glad! The Supremacy of God in Missions* (Grand Rapids: Baker Academic, 2010).

came upon them and they preached the gospel of Jesus Christ. They then baptized new believers and gathered them into churches.[11] As they preached and taught, they laid the foundation of the church (Eph 2:20), which has been entrusted to us in the Bible (1 Thess 2:13; 2 Tim 3:16).

This claim about the Holy Spirit working by ordinary means has long been understood by Protestants to be what the Bible teaches. This is no novel doctrine but is basic Protestant teaching. The 2LCF states this: "The grace of faith, whereby the elect are enabled to believe to the saving of their souls, is the work of the Spirit of Christ in their hearts, and is ordinarily wrought by the ministry of the Word; by which also, and by the administration of baptism and the Lord's supper, prayer, and other means appointed of God, it is increased and strengthened."[12]

The Christian church has long concurred on these ordinary means because they are the consistently observed pattern of the work of the Holy Spirit. The Holy Spirit loves Jesus, and he loves to witness to him. He is on mission to proclaim Jesus to the hearts of men (John 15:26–16:15). In every instance in which we read that the Holy Spirit has filled a person, we see that person respond by proclaiming Christ (Luke 1:41–43, 67–69; 2:25–32; Acts 2:5–47; 4:8–12). The Holy Spirit is on mission to proclaim Christ to the hearts of men through his appointed means.

As Luke records, when the church was filled with the Holy Spirit, they preached Christ with boldness: "And when they had prayed, the place in which they were gathered together was shaken, and they were all *filled with the Holy Spirit and continued to speak the word of God* with boldness" (Acts 4:31, emphasis added). The Holy Spirit works through clear preaching of the Word of God. The Holy Spirit puts the treasure of the gospel of Christ in jars of clay like us to show that the surpassing power belongs to God and not us (2 Cor 4:7).

---

11 See chapters 5–6 for more.
12 2LCF 14.1. See also WCF 14.1.

APPLICATION

I (Chad) was once engaged in a debate regarding methodology in missions.[13] As I pressed this point regarding the ordinary means through which the Holy Spirit works, I was accused of "putting God into a box" and not sufficiently trusting in God's ability to do whatever he wants. I replied that we were considering the wrong question; the question is not what the Holy Spirit is *able* to do but what the Holy Spirit *commands us* to do. He can do whatever he wants—he spoke through a donkey, after all (Numbers 22). However, we are not going to airlift donkeys into unreached language groups and pray the Holy Spirit miraculously speaks through them! Rather, it is necessary that we attend to the work the Lord has given us to do in his Word because it, not our innovative methods, is the power of God for the salvation of his people everywhere (Rom 1:16). It is not wrong to expect or pray fervently for God to exercise his power in incredible ways, and we should be slow to impute malicious intent to those inclined to hope or pray accordingly. But we cannot test the Lord by neglecting the beautiful simplicity of our duty to preach Christ under the guise of giving God "room" to work.

The Holy Spirit is absolutely necessary to our missions efforts. Apart from the work of the Holy Spirit, our words fall to the ground. Further, no one will benefit from the redemptive work of Christ apart from the application of that work by the Holy Spirit (1 Cor 2:10–14; 12:3). Counterintuitively, the Holy Spirit does the extraordinary work of converting men to Christ through the ordinary means of preaching. This truth does not change as we cross geopolitical borders and language barriers. We continue to bear the responsibility to communicate the gospel clearly, and rather ordinarily, in the language of a particular people group. The Holy Spirit is pleased to work through those means. We remain utterly dependent on him to give individuals ears to hear, eyes to see, and hearts to believe. Without him, we can do nothing. John Owen wrote about Christ's gift of the Holy Spirit: "He would

---

13 More on this in chapter 6.

have them look neither for assistance in their work, nor success unto it, but from the promised Spirit alone; and lets them know, also, that by his aid they should be enabled to carry their testimony of him to the uttermost parts of the earth. And herein lay, and herein doth lie, the foundation of the ministry of the church, as also its continuance and efficacy."[14]

STUDY QUESTIONS

1. What is the mission of the Holy Spirit, according to our Lord Jesus? (See Luke 24:47–49; John 14:26; 15:26–27; 16:7–15; Acts 1:8.)

2. How does the Holy Spirit's pleasure to work through the ordinary means of preaching the gospel, prayer, and the ordinances (baptism and the Lord's Supper) shape our understanding of the missionary's task?

3. If the Bible never commands us to look for a "new wind of the Holy Spirit" in how he carries out his mission, what do you think drives our desire for that? What are some godly or ungodly motivations for expecting the miraculous? What does our dissatisfaction with the ordinary work of the Holy Spirit imply about our judgment of his wisdom in ministry?

4. Are we "putting God in a box" when we employ the ordinary means he has given us? Why does patiently and obediently exercising these ordinary means actually demonstrate faith in the Holy Spirit to do the work?

5. How do we assess claims of new and extraordinary works of the Holy Spirit? What is the standard by which we judge those claims? (See 2LCF 1.10.) How is it loving to hold our missionaries to that standard?

---

14 Owen, *The Works of John Owen*, 191.

6. If the Holy Spirit has given us ordinary means that require us to learn the language and culture of a people at a level of fluency so we can properly exercise these means among them, what sort of skills does this imply missionaries must be equipped with? What responsibility does the church retain in ensuring our missionaries have these skills and are employing them faithfully?

5

THE CHURCH CHRIST IS BUILDING IN ALL NATIONS

*I will build my church, and the gates of hell
shall not prevail against it.*
Matthew 16:18

"I like Jesus, but I don't like organized religion."

"My faith is personal; I don't need church to connect with God."

"Jesus came to start a movement, not a new religion. Buildings and institutions get in the way of the personal relationship God wants with us."

Doubtless we have all heard statements like these as we seek to follow Christ in the postmodern, de-churched culture of the West. The average Westerner considers religion a matter of the heart, to remain safely sealed off from the public realm. Many profess an affinity for Jesus of Nazareth; few are willing to publicly align themselves with a local church body. In this way, the church has fallen on hard times.

We have come to expect such critiques from the secular world. Now consider this statement:

> Does a non-Christian have to come into Western Christianity to come to Christ? Must Buddhists, Hindus, and Muslims become Christians in order to belong to Christ? Do they have to be incorporated into church organizations that are utterly alien to their re-

ligious traditions? Do they have to call themselves Christians? Do they have to adopt Christian customs and rites which are necessarily Western? . . . Millions are worshipping Jesus in India, but they are not being baptized because they don't want to join the Western fold. They would have to leave their Hindu world. Millions of Indians are following Jesus but have not taken baptism and committed cultural suicide and entered a Western alien fold.[1]

These objections to formal church membership come not from a secular sociological analyst or a new age spiritual guru convinced that the way of Jesus is a thread woven through all religious traditions but from a leading evangelical missiologist. Elsewhere the same missiologist reduces the idea of a "congregation"—a "formal incorporation into a bounded religious membership with an historic Christian legacy"—to an "ecclesial structure [that] emerged in the socio-religious context of the Roman world."[2] In other words, the church as an organized institution is a construct of the West and should be questioned.

These critiques of the church are not uncommon within mainstream missions thought. Many such critiques derive from a broader school of thought advocating so-called insider movements, which promotes that individuals converted to Christ within other major world religions retain their old socioreligious identity (e.g., Muslim, Hindu) and attempt to follow Jesus within the framework of their original religion for fear of losing their network for relational evangelism.[3] Thus, a new follower of Christ is instructed to avoid association with a separate Christian community and instead to identify as Muslim, worship

---

[1] Brad Gill, "03/22/15 - AM Service – Missions Conference Speaker" First Baptist Church of St. Johns, March 22, 2015, http://stjohnsfbc.com/sermons.html.

[2] Brad Gill, "A Christology for Frontier Mission: A Missiological Study of Colossians," *International Journal of Frontier Missiology*, no. 34:1–4 (2017): 100.

[3] Rebecca Lewis writes of these movements: "Believers retain their identity as members of their socio-religious community while living under the Lordship of Jesus Christ and the authority of the Bible" ("Insider Movements: Retaining Identity and Preserving Community," *Perspectives on the World Christian Movement*, eds. Ralph Winter and Steven Hawthorne, 4th ed. [Pasadena, CA: William Carey, 2009], 673).

in the mosque on Fridays, read the Qur'an, eat halal, and perhaps even continue to confess Muhammad as a prophet.[4]

Insider movements are just one example of the devaluing of the church in evangelical thought. From North America to the frontiers of world missions, pragmatism presses a biblical understanding of the local church into the margins of the Christian life. But before we can understand this critical moment in the modern missionary movement, we must first build a positive theology of the church on the foundation of Scripture.

DEFINING THE CHURCH

As a missionary mobilizer, I (Alex) often officiate doctrinal interviews with our long-term missionary candidates, walking them through each fountainhead of Christian theology to verify that they are equipped for cross-cultural service. When I reach ecclesiology (the doctrine of the church), I often begin by describing the sort of encounters described at the beginning of this chapter—accounts of conversations with individuals who feel as though "Jesus is for me, but church gatherings are not." I ask interviewees to consider how they would respond. Why should someone who claims to follow Christ submit themselves to a local church? The answers come: "You need the accountability of other believers to grow in your Christian walk," or, "Without hearing regular preaching, you'll never mature," or even, "You need a place to use your spiritual gifts to serve others."

What is wrong with these responses? They all revolve around *me*! Most Christian replies to postmodern objections to the local church concern the church as an *instrumental means*—something I use in the

---

4 Missiologist "John Travis" (pseudonym) describes "a community of Muslims who follow Jesus yet remain culturally and officially Muslim," and these "believers are viewed as Muslims by the Muslim community and think of themselves as Muslims who follow Isa the Messiah" ("The C1–C6 Spectrum: A Practical Tool for Defining Six Types of 'Christ–centered Communities' Found in the Muslim Context," in *Perspectives on the World Christian Movement*, eds. Ralph Winter and Steven Hawthorne, 4th ed. [Pasadena, CA: William Carey, 2009], 665).

project of my own spiritual growth—rather than first addressing the *ontology* of the church—what the church *is* and why. These answers, while all technically true, are more reflective of our individualistic culture than of the fullness of biblical teaching concerning the body of Christ.

The church is not an appendage to a gospel message that is otherwise purely focused on personal spirituality; rather, the church is a product of the gospel itself. Consider how the apostle Paul describes the action of God the Father through the redemptive work of Christ: "He has delivered us from the domain of darkness and transferred us to the kingdom of his beloved Son, in whom we have redemption, the forgiveness of sins" (Col 1:13–14). God's work in salvation itself yields a community of the redeemed. Since God through Christ is rescuing men and women out of the domain of sin, death, and hell, it necessarily follows that he is transferring them into a new and better kingdom. And because each believer is intimately united to Christ in salvation, this counter-community of the redeemed also enjoys inseparable unity within itself.

From the moment the first gospel promise was given in Genesis 3:15 that the seed of the woman would crush the head of Satan, those with faith in the promise existed as an objective community in the eyes of God, who had covenanted in eternity past not only to open a general way of salvation but to himself save a *particular* assembly of people (Eph 1:11; Titus 2:14; Rev 5:9). This single people of God includes all true believers in history, even prior to the formal inauguration of the church under the new covenant on the day of Pentecost (Acts 2), and spans nations, cultures, and languages. Hence, throughout church history, Christians have confessed belief in "the holy catholic church" ("catholic" meaning universal) and "the communion of saints" (referring to the spiritual unity of all God's people, including both believers on earth and departed saints in heaven).[5]

---

5 The Apostles' Creed, c. AD 542 ed.

THE CHURCH: UNIVERSAL AND LOCAL

"Think global; act local." This common adage, though now clichéd in the world of politics and social action, bears relevance to our understanding of the church. We may consider the church in two respects: global and local.

Scripture bears out that God has a special people who are the objects of his redemptive work. Yet anyone who has spent time in a local church knows that not all who profess to be a part of this body have the root of the matter in them. False professors of faith come and go, and the physical gathering of individuals in the local church is an imperfect outpost of the true, regenerate people of God. Christians have thus historically recognized a distinction between the *invisible* or *universal church*, the whole of God's people spanning time and space and composed of all the elect, and the *visible church*, which is manifest in *local churches*. The 2LCF describes this distinction thus:

> The catholic or universal church, which (with respect to the internal work of the Spirit and truth of grace) may be called invisible, consists of the whole number of the elect, that have been, are, or shall be gathered into one, under Christ, the head thereof; and is the spouse, the body, the fulness of him that filleth all in all. All persons throughout the world, professing the faith of the gospel, and obedience unto God by Christ according unto it, not destroying their own profession by any errors everting the foundation, or unholiness of conversation, are and may be called visible saints; and of such ought all particular congregations to be constituted.[6]

To understand both the nature of the church and the church-centered nature of missions, we must explore the church both as it exists universally and as it is expressed locally.

---

6 2LCF 26:1–2. Presbyterians broaden the visible church to include the children of believers as well. The Westminster Confession of Faith reads, "The visible Church . . . consists of all those throughout the world that profess the true religion; and of their children" (25:2). Without dismissing the significance of this disagreement, we may recognize that, whichever view one takes, both views grapple with the reality that the visible church is inevitably mixed (consisting of both regenerate and unregenerate) while the invisible church is pure (consisting only of the elect).

A People for His Name

John Piper has famously remarked that "missions exists because worship doesn't."[7] Missions, in other words, is a means to an end. God's goal—and ours—is that the whole earth would be filled with his glory just as the waters cover the sea (Isa 11:9; Hab 2:14). This was the original goal of the command given to Adam to take dominion of the creation, be fruitful, and fill the earth (Gen 1:28)—a goal forfeited by Adam but fulfilled in Christ. This goal will only be realized once every corner of the globe is populated with people who are turned back from rebellion and remade in the image of Christ (see Col 3:10; Eph 4:24) to reflect God's glory in worship—a redeemed race set apart to declare the excellencies of him who called them, a people made to declare his name (1 Pet 2:9). And God has promised this will happen among every nation (Isa 43:7; Rev 5:9).

Another way of saying that God's goal in history and redemption is global worship is that God's goal in history and redemption is *the church*. From the earliest recorded human history, when pagan mankind attempted to get glory for itself through the construction of the tower of Babel, God's response was to "make a name" for a single man named Abram in such a way that *God* would receive all the glory (Gen 11:4; 12:2). This returned to God his rightful glory through the covenant community that would flow from one man's bloodline. The covenant family of God is to be a missionary people, spreading the knowledge of the true God to all the nations and ultimately giving rise to the Messiah (Gen 12:3; Deut 4:6–8; 7:6). When this people had grown into a nation, they were to "declare his glory among the nations" (Ps 96:3), and their temple was in turn to be a "house of prayer for all peoples" (Isa 56:7). In all this, it was God's intent that all the peoples of the earth would praise him (Ps 67:3–5). This purpose is fulfilled in

---

7 Piper, *Let the Nations Be Glad!*, 17. Piper expounds, "Missions is not the ultimate goal of the church. Worship is. . . . Worship is ultimate, not missions, because God is ultimate, not man. When this age is over, and the countless millions of the redeemed fall on their faces before the throne of God, missions will be no more. It is a temporary necessity. But worship abides forever."

Christ as he gathers his people from all nations and ethnicities and not Jews only (Eph 3:6). Christ redeems to himself a global people to proclaim his excellencies (1 Pet 2:9).

A Visible People

But missions does not just exist to perpetuate an amorphous global movement. The line of the above-cited confession concerning "particular congregations" constituted of "visible saints" is of acute concern to missionary workers. All God's elect compose the invisible church, but we are not to content ourselves in belonging to this global community without that spiritual reality touching down into our own lives. For the goal of global worship to be realized, particular churches must be formed as local outposts of Christ's kingdom with flesh-and-blood members: "Those thus called, he commandeth to walk together in particular societies, or churches, for their mutual edification, and the due performance of that public worship, which he requireth of them in the world."[8] The confession continues,

> The members of these churches are saints by calling, visibly manifesting and evidencing (in and by their profession and walking) their obedience unto that call of Christ; and *do willingly consent to walk together*, according to the appointment of Christ; *giving up themselves to the Lord, and one to another*, by the will of God, in professed subjection to the ordinances of the Gospel. . . . As *all believers are bound to join themselves to particular churches*, when and where they have opportunity so to do; so all that are admitted unto the privileges of a church, are also under the censures and government thereof, according to the rule of Christ.[9]

While God's goal of global worship entails more than the establishment of believing congregations, it cannot mean less. This is not just the assertion seventeenth-century Europeans forced on the text of Scripture but is the direct biblical teaching itself.

---

8 2LCF 26:5.
9 2LCF 26:6, 12, emphasis added.

Both testaments of Scripture bear witness that God ordains and commands regular, visible, public, local gathering of those who profess the faith. Even under the old covenant, the people of God came together as an "assembly" or "congregation." The Septuagint, the Greek translation of the Old Testament, and the New Testament both use the term *ekklēsia* and its related words to refer to the gathered congregation of God's covenant people.[10] After the Jews' return from exile, we see the pattern established of the *ekklēsia* gathering for public prayer, worship, Scripture reading, and elaboration upon the meaning of the Scriptures (Neh 8:1–8). To be cut off from the *ekklēsia* was considered a curse (Deut 23:1–2, 8; Neh 13:1). As the Jewish *diaspora* persisted after the exile and worshipers of Yahweh were spread throughout the Persian, Greek, and Roman empires, the Jews' inability to access a temple in Jerusalem resulted in the birth of the synagogue system, which later became a blueprint for Christian local churches.[11]

In the New Testament, Jesus modeled the observance of public worship, making it his custom to attend the Jewish synagogue each Sabbath (Luke 4:16). When Jesus ascended, his followers met together for prayer (Acts 1:14) and continued to gather regularly for teaching, fellowship, praise, mutual benevolence, and the enjoyment of the ordinances of baptism and the Lord's Supper (2:42–47). This covenant-renewing gathering took place in particular on the first day of the week, marking the Lord's Day—a new "sabbath" day to mark the new creation inaugurated at the resurrection of Christ, the second Adam (see Acts 20:7; 1 Cor 16:2; Rev 1:10). Those who persisted in unrepentant sin were to be excluded from the assembly (Matt 18:17; 1 Cor 5:4–5),

---

10 These biblical citations can be multiplied and are not exhaustive. Consider Deut 4:10; 9:10; 10:4; 18:16; Josh 8:35; 1 Kgs 8:14, 22, 55, 65; 1 Chr 28:2; 29:1, 10, 20; 2 Chr 1:3, 5; 6:3; 7:8; 20:5, 14; 23:3; 29:28, 31, 32; 30:2, 4, 13, 17, 23–25.

11 The English word "synagogue" is a loan word from the Greek *sunagōgē*, which is translated variously throughout the New Testament as "assembly" or "synagogue" and stems from the verb "to gather" (*sunagō*). In the New Testament usage, *sunagōgē* can refer to Jewish synagogues or by analogy to Christian churches (possibly in Jas 2:2). The synagogue model, a by-product of the exile and dispersion, was a divine providence preparing the people of God for the new covenant era in which true worship would no longer be centered geographically on the temple in Jerusalem.

while faithful believers were encouraged to continue gathering with perseverance, even amid persecution, for fellowship with the Lord and mutual edification among themselves (Heb 10:24–25).

While the Lord knows those who are his (2 Tim 2:19), he also ordains that his people gather, and that when they do so, he is really, spiritually present in their midst (Matt 18:20; Rev 2:1). It is true we are saved by Christ alone through faith alone and that faith is individual and personal. Yet we only receive Christ in the preaching of the gospel, which finds its home in the Word and sacrament of the church. In this sense, we can stoutly affirm the words of Cyprian of Carthage: "He can no longer have God for his Father, who has not the Church for his mother."[12] It makes no sense to speak of God's work in the world to redeem those he loves without speaking in distinct terms about a visible, identifiable Christian community that meets physically and regularly to worship, fellowship, and celebrate their covenant with their Lord.

Until now, we have not yet discussed the particulars of a biblical church. Yet, as demonstrated in the introduction to this chapter, the task of the missionary depends on knowing a healthy church from an unhealthy one—or a false one. For that, we must turn to the words of Jesus.

THE CHURCH CHRIST IS BUILDING

Contrary to what is often claimed in modern times, the church as an institution was not a later invention of the apostle Paul or the post-apostolic period but was the express design of Jesus himself. A key text for our understanding is Matthew 16:13–19:

> Now when Jesus came into the district of Caesarea Philippi, he asked his disciples, "Who do people say that the Son of Man is?" And they said, "Some say John the Baptist, others say Elijah, and others Jeremiah or one of the prophets." He said to them, "But who do you say that I am?" Simon Peter replied, "You are the Christ, the

---

12 Cyprian of Carthage, *On the Unity of the Church*, trans. Robert Ernest Wallis, from *Ante-Nicene Fathers*, vol. 5, ed. Alexander Roberts, James Donaldson, and A. Cleveland Coxe (Buffalo, NY: Christian Literature, 1886). Revised and edited for New Advent by Kevin Knight, http://www.newadvent.org/fathers/050701.htm.

Son of the living God." And Jesus answered him, "Blessed are you, Simon Bar-Jonah! For flesh and blood has not revealed this to you, but my Father who is in heaven. And I tell you, you are Peter, and on this rock I will build my church, and the gates of hell shall not prevail against it. I will give you the keys of the kingdom of heaven, and whatever you bind on earth shall be bound in heaven, and whatever you loose on earth shall be loosed in heaven."

From this crucial passage spring four nonnegotiable elements of the church. The first three correspond with what Reformed theologians have recognized as the marks of a true church.[13]

Mark #1: The Preaching of the Word

Consider the scene. Jesus, at the height of his popularity, asks his disciples who the public says he is. "John the Baptist, Elijah, Jeremiah, or some other Old Testament prophet," they reply. Jesus responds with an emphatic interrogative: "But who do *you* say I am?"—addressing all the disciples. Peter responds on behalf of the group: "You are the Christ, the Son of the living God." His response is the response of gospel faith. The apostles knew that Jesus was not just a prophet but God incarnate—"My Lord and my God!" as Thomas would exclaim after the resurrection (John 20:28). Jesus blesses Peter, noting that his faith is a gift from God the Father. On this faith foundation, Christ will build his *ekklēsia*, which will triumph over the gates of hades. And in this faith, Peter is given the apostolic authority to recognize the remittance or retainment of sin-guilt.

Unfortunately, many evangelicals only deal with this significant text in addressing the Roman Catholic Church's claim that Peter is here established by Christ as the first pope.[14] Many Protestants point

---

[13] "The marks by which the true Church is known are these: If the pure doctrine of the gospel is preached therein; if it maintains the pure administration of the sacraments as instituted by Christ; if church discipline is exercised in punishing sin," Belgic Confession (1561), Article 29.

[14] The Roman Catholic Catechism reads, "The Lord made St. Peter the visible foundation of his Church. He entrusted the keys of the Church to him. The bishop of the Church of Rome, successor to St. Peter, is 'head of the college of bishops, the Vicar of Christ and Pastor of the universal Church on earth' (CIC, can. 331)" (*Cat-*

out that Peter's confession of faith is to be the church's foundation rather than Peter's office itself. The true church is built on the gospel—the "good confession" (1 Tim 6:12–13)—and not a single man.[15] To further demonstrate the point, later in the chapter when Peter denies that Christ will have to suffer, Jesus sharply rebukes him: "Get behind me, Satan!" (Matt 6:23). In other words, Peter is a "rock" to the degree that he makes the good confession, but when he breaks the faith, he is regarded as a practical devil.

From this first part of the text, we see that the church Christ is building is a church that is *publicly confessional*. Christ is publicly preached, believed, and confessed. We do not merely hold private opinions or interpretations of subjective spiritual experiences, nor does a local church consist in a pre-existing community developing a vague interest in a man named Jesus. Peter did not merely "ask Jesus into his heart"; he verbally announced his allegiance to Christ. We, in turn, together verbally confess the same faith as the apostles. This is truly the only type of apostolic succession that matters—a succession of doctrine, not office. The true church thus exists, first, wherever the Word of God is rightly preached and believed.

Mark #2: The Administration of the Sacraments

The preaching and public confession of the biblical gospel is a necessary mark of a true local church, but it is not the only mark. Like Peter, we confess this faith not only through inward assent to a series of propositions but through a public declaration—one visibly expressed in the act of baptism, which lies at the heart of the church's missionary

---

echism of the Catholic Church, 936, accessed January 2, 2021, https://www.vatican.va/archive/ccc_css/archive/catechism/p123a9p4.htm).

15 It is not altogether false, however, that Peter seems to occupy a lead role among the apostles. Moreover, the singular pronouns that follow in Matt.16:19 ("I will give you the keys . . . whatever you bind . . . whatever you loose") are singular (referring presumably to Peter) rather than plural. This is not a problem for Protestants, considering that in at least one parallel text (e.g., John 20:23), the pronouns are plural, referring to all the apostles. This concept of the keys of the kingdom will be explored later in this chapter.

mandate ("Go therefore and make disciples of all nations, baptizing them" [Matt 28:19]). This leads to our second recognition: that the church is also a community of those who have publicly identified themselves with the Lord in baptism and who center their fellowship around the Lord's Supper, or Communion. These identifying activities of the church are the two *sacraments* or *ordinances* given to the people of God in the new covenant.[16]

In Acts 2, we learn that the new covenant is both marked out by the initiatory sign of baptism (undertaken by individuals making a profession of faith) and centered on regular participation in the Communion meal: "And Peter said to them, 'Repent and be baptized every one of you in the name of Jesus Christ for the forgiveness of your sins.' . . . So *those who received his word were baptized*, and there were added that day about three thousand souls. And they devoted themselves to the apostles' teaching and the fellowship, *to the breaking of bread* and the prayers" (vv. 38, 41–42, emphasis added).

These sacraments are not "works" required for salvation in addition to faith. Neither are they dead memorials whose only benefit is in the psychology of the participant. Rather, they are a "visible word"—grace-laced symbols communicating the same gospel message and grace for our sanctification that we received by faith alone for our justification.[17] Christ is spiritually present with his people through the sacraments.

---

16 The term "sacrament" does not imply some magical power in the bare act but derives from the Latin *sacrāmentum*, used by older translators (e.g., Jerome in the Vulgate) to translate the Greek *mystērion* ("mysteries"). In the New Testament, a "mystery" is not a magical secret but a divine truth formerly hidden now made known in the Christian age. Many Baptists prefer "ordinance" because it avoids misunderstanding and emphasizes the command of Christ. The authors use both terms interchangeably.

17 The Protestant Reformers were fond of this language over against the Roman Catholic view that placed the power of the sacrament in the act itself. John Calvin, citing Augustine, writes, "Augustine calls a sacrament a *visible word* (August. in Joann. Hom. 89), because it represents the promises of God as in a picture, and places them in our view in a graphic bodily form (August. cont. Faust. Lib. 19)." (*Institutes of the Christian Religion*, trans. Henry Beveridge [Grand Rapids: Eerdmans, 1989], accessed August 26, 2020, https://www.ccel.org/ccel/calvin/institutes/institutes.vi.xv.html.)

Thus, to require believers to be baptized publicly or come to the Table is not to impose any Western cultural tradition. It is simply following Scripture. Moreover, the sacraments are inherently *counter-cultural*—requiring believers to publicly identify themselves with the culture of God's kingdom and stand out from the world. In baptism, we, with Peter, confess our faith publicly, and in the Lord's Supper we "proclaim the Lord's death until he comes" (1 Cor 11:26). Far from Jewish or Greco-Roman cultural baggage, the ordinances of the church stand as tools of cross-cultural missionary witness from age to age.

Mark #3: The Discipline of the Church

When Peter confesses the faith, Jesus blesses him, noting that "flesh and blood" did not reveal it to him but the "Father who is in heaven" (Matt 16:17). We are reminded that the invisible, or catholic, church consists of all the true people of God in all the world who are known only to God—his elect. The members of the universal church are "called to belong to Jesus Christ" (Rom 1:6), drawn by the Father (John 6:44), and chosen "according to the foreknowledge of God the Father" (1 Pet 1:1–2). The exact identity of God's chosen is known only to him (see Deut 29:29); we can only judge a person's spiritual state by his profession of faith and personal conduct. Nevertheless, local church assemblies—which are always, inevitably composed of both true and false converts—are called to be holy.

God has thus entrusted to local churches the stewardship of recognizing his true people. Despite our limitations, discharging this duty of discernment safeguards the public witness and holiness of the church. So, Jesus further elucidates, "I will give you the keys of the kingdom of heaven, and whatever you bind on earth shall be bound in heaven, and whatever you loose on earth shall be loosed in heaven" (Matt 16:19). Jesus is not giving the apostle authority to unilaterally dispense forgiveness of sins; a better translation would read "shall *have been* bound . . . shall *have been* loosed," meaning that earth follows heaven.[18] God's

---

[18] This translation, though doubted by some, reflects that the participial phrases in question are in the future perfect passive tense, and is reflected in the New Ameri-

decree comes first, and earth responds in recognition of the decision. This translates directly into our understanding of church discipline at a local level.

As the leaders of the church preach the gospel of forgiveness, sinners are loosed from their bonds. Conversely, those who bear witness by their words or by unrepentant sin that they do not belong to Christ lose their right to participate in the Christian fellowship and are to be regarded as outsiders (Matt 18:17). In one such situation in Corinth, the apostle Paul makes explicit that this means those engaged in unrepentant sin must be disfellowshipped (1 Cor 5:4–5). "[It is] those inside the church whom you are to judge. . . . 'Purge the evil person from among you'" (vv. 12–13). That the church is to be holy does not mean it is perfect; even the "purest churches under heaven are subject to mixture and error."[19] This does not, however, absolve us of our obligation to keep the church pure.

This clear biblical teaching also implies that some formal practice of church membership must be practiced. Excommunication means nothing without defined membership. We read of Pentecost that "there were added that day about three thousand souls" (Acts 2:41). Clearly there must be a way to ascertain which souls are to be counted among the church and which are not. Here again we see not a Western form but a plain, biblical example not exclusively bound to a particular historical circumstance. Through both positive discipline (preaching, evangelism, counseling) and negative discipline (rebuke, correction, excommunication), the apostles and the church today wield the keys of entry and exit from God's visible kingdom on earth.

Mark #4: The Mission of the Church

Theologians and church leaders have historically recognized the preaching of the Word and the right administration of the sacraments as the irreducible ingredients of a local church and the practice of biblical

---

can Standard Bible, Christian Standard Bible, and Berean Literal Bible.
19   2LCF, 26.3.

church discipline as their necessary outgrowth. But Matthew 16 leads us to enumerate one more key element: namely, that the church is *sent*.

After Jesus renames Simon as "Peter" ("rock"), he vows: "I will build my church" (Matt 16:18). First note in Christ's promise the juxtaposition of "build" and "church." We might expect Jesus to use these words together, since we are prone to think of church as a physical building. But when we consider that *ekklēsia* means *congregation* or *assembly*, Jesus's choice of the word "build" stands out. We might perhaps expect to read that Christ will "gather" his congregation or "call" his assembly—verbs that have precedent in Matthew's Gospel.[20] Instead, the verb chosen is "build"—*oikodomeō*—a compound word stemming from "house" (*oíkos*) and referring most often to literal construction. Jesus is not simply amassing a movement of followers but constructing a house (see 2 Sam 7:16; Luke 1:33). The church is something *solid*.

Jesus continues: "The gates of hell shall not prevail against it." Often, we are conditioned to believe that Christ will return someday to an embattled, beleaguered church that failed its mission and was nearly stamped out by the global forces of evil. But gates, it must be noted, are defensive, not offensive, mechanisms. It is the church, not the kingdom of darkness, that is making territorial advances in the present age. Jesus spoke these words in Caesarea Philippi, a locale dedicated to the pagan deity Zeus and situated near the biblical Mount Hermon, associated in Jewish thought with dark spiritual forces that enslaved Gentile nations in idolatry. Jesus intends for the church to march victoriously throughout the world, storming hell's gates and loosing the pagan world from Satan's grip. The principalities and powers of the world are to be overcome through the preaching of the gospel. Daniel foresaw this global triumph of the gospel in Nebuchadnezzar's dream (Dan 2:35), and such readers as Augustine of Hippo (AD 354–430) have read Daniel's interpretation as a promise of the New Testament church.[21]

---

20 See 18:20; 20:16; 22:10, 14, for instance.
21 Augustine: "It is that mountain [the church] which, according to Daniel's vision, grew from a very small 'stone' till it overtook the kingdoms of the earth and grew to such a size that it 'filled the face of the earth'" ("Exposition on Psalm 43.4," *Expositions of the Psalms*, https://www.newadvent.org/fathers/1801043.htm).

Moreover, Jesus plundered hades itself—the abode of the dead—securing in his resurrection the resurrection of all believers into the heavenly presence of God (see Ps 16:10–11; 1 Cor 15:23; 2 Cor 5:8; Eph 4:8–10). The church is victorious because Jesus is victorious! In turn, Jesus grants us to share in his mission: "As the Father has sent me, even so I am sending you" (John 20:21). The bride of Christ participates in the mission of her Husband by making disciples of all nations.

APPLICATION

In the beginning of this chapter, we considered current trends in missiology compelling us to deconstruct the concept of the local church. These methods, often undertaken with the sincerest evangelistic motives, obscure Christ's *ekklēsia* and render it indistinguishable from any other religious or social class. But rather than deconstruct the church, Jesus Christ promises to *build* his church among the nations. The local church is both the subject and the object of Christ's mission. His mission in the world is to assemble the church, and the church's work in the world is to accomplish the work of mission.

This truth bears at least four implications for the missionary:

- First, the Great Commission requires the establishment of visible local churches among the peoples of the world.
- Second, the Great Commission requires that these churches share in the core marks of a church—*the ministry of Word and sacrament* and *biblical discipline*—yet this does *not* constrain every church in the world to look identical. Culture, language, musical style, dress, and location will all vary by context. Some churches will own buildings; others will meet in homes. Scripture gives us clear boundaries for what constitutes a church, yet these boundaries give ample room for healthy contextualization and adaptation to circumstance.[22]

---

22 2LCF 1:6.

- Third, the fulfillment of the Great Commission requires the establishment of qualified nationals as elders and deacons. Just as the apostle Paul sought to appoint local elders in every church he planted (Acts 14:23) and commissioned men like Timothy to entrust the teaching to "faithful men, who will be able to teach others also" (2 Tim 2:2), so the missionary's task is not complete until the new church is built up with indigenous leadership.

- Fourth, the Great Commission is the responsibility of local churches. The church at Antioch sent the first missionaries (Acts 13:1–3), and it remains for visible local bodies today to commission cross-cultural workers. We are not permitted to be lone gunslingers for Christ. No one can "call" themselves. To be a missionary is to be "sent" by the church in a similar sense in which the apostles were commissioned by Christ. This implies a relationship of partnership and accountability between the sending church and the missionary.

To devote ourselves to the worldwide building of the church is not to resign ourselves to an outdated, traditionalistic model of missions. It is, rather, to join Christ on his quest in which the gates of hell will not prevail against his assembled saints. As we commit ourselves to what his Word has prescribed for the local assembly, he will victoriously gather all nations into his covenant people.

STUDY QUESTIONS

1. Suppose you are inviting a nominal Christian neighbor or co-worker to your church. How do you explain why it is necessary for Christians to join themselves to a local church?

2. What is God's goal for the world? What role does the church play regarding the accomplishment of global worship?

3. Consider the missions organizations and international Christian nonprofits with which you may be familiar. Do they prioritize church planting and strengthen existing churches? Why or why not?

4. Read the *Serampore Form of Agreement* (1805) published by William Carey and his missionary team in India. (The full text can be easily found online.) Note article 8, paragraph 2. Why did the group think it their duty "to advise the native brethren who may be formed in separate churches, to choose their pastors and deacons from amongst their own countrymen, that the word may be statedly preached, and the ordinances of Christ administered, in each church, by the native minister, as much as possible, without the interference of the missionary"? Do you think this is biblical or unbiblical? Why or why not? What are the advantages of following this approach?

6

The Apostles' Commission to Proclaim Christ in All Nations

Thus it is written, that the Christ should suffer and on the third day rise from the dead, and that repentance for the forgiveness of sins should be proclaimed in his name to all nations, beginning from Jerusalem. You are witnesses of these things. And behold, I am sending the promise of my Father upon you. But stay in the city until you are clothed with power from on high.
Luke 24:46–49

A few years ago, I (Chad) wrote a short article published by Radius International critiquing disciple-making movements (DMM), a methodology which currently enjoys near-ubiquitous popularity in the mainstream evangelical missions community.[1] Little was I prepared for the cascading effect of controversy sparked by that article. Soon, I was invited to participate in a debate with the president of a major missions organization centering on whether Scripture calls believers to practice DMM methods.[2] I assumed the negative position, while my opponent held that Scripture left the area of methodology open-ended, allowing

---

[1] See Chad Vegas, "A Brief Guide to DMM: Defining and Evaluating the Ideas Impacting Missions Today," Radius International, June 11, 2018, https://www.radiusinternational.org/a-brief-guide-to-dmm.

[2] The full debate can be found on the following web page: Brad Buser, "Church Planting Movement Model vs the Proclamation Model," Radius International, December 17, 2018, https://www.radiusinternational.org/church-planting-movement-model-and-the-proclamational-model-debate.

DMM as one of many conceivable options for missionaries. The debate lasted more than two hours and in the years since has continued to generate no small amount of contention. Yet a single, consistent theme has marked the entire conversation: well-meaning, biblically literate missions practitioners repeatedly stumble over my assertion that God's Word necessitates *one* particular methodology.

Before specific methodologies like DMM or its counterpart, church-planting movements (CPM), can be analyzed, we must determine where we stand on the issue of methodology in general. Does the Word of God commend—or perhaps command—*one* method? At first, one may be inclined to answer no. Many in the missions community are taught that while the Christian faith is a matter of truth and error, methodology in missions and ministry is effectively neutral. Methodology is like Switzerland—it takes no side in a disagreement; it is, consistent with its nature, removed altogether from the conflict. Yet, as we have contended throughout this book, the tactics and practices one carries into ministry are always *necessarily* birthed from one's theology, consciously or unconsciously. To return to Petrus van Mastricht's dictum cited in the introduction, doctrine and practice walk together. We maintain that Scripture in effect *does* teach gospel workers to engage in a particular method, to the exclusion of other methods.

Our purpose in this chapter is to demonstrate how Jesus, in his final command to his apostles, commended this particular missions methodology to his apostles, who then proceeded to follow this methodology throughout the New Testament. We will first consider Christ's clear instruction to the apostles (doctrine) and then their repeated pattern of obedience (practice).

CHRIST'S COMMISSION

The account of Jesus's final words to his apostles in Luke's Gospel provided the doctrine that the apostles then consistently practiced. As Jesus spoke to the apostles in the upper room on the evening of his resurrection, "he opened their minds to understand the Scriptures"

(Luke 24:45). He proclaimed himself to be the fulfillment of the Old Testament prophecies of the Messiah who would bring reconciliation between God and man (vv. 44–46). His sin-atoning work on the cross and his life-giving resurrection from the grave are the means by which men are forgiven their sins and justified before God.[3] This is the gospel (doctrine) that Jesus then promised his apostles would be proclaimed to all nations (v. 47). Further, Jesus commanded his apostles—witnesses of his life, death, and resurrection—to stay in Jerusalem until he sent the Holy Spirit upon them to empower them for their gospel mission (vv. 48–49; Acts 1:8).

We see three truths in this short narrative that shape the pattern and practice of the disciples in the Acts of the Apostles.[4] First, we are given the *gospel message* that will be made known (Luke 24:44–46). The message will focus on man's need to be reconciled to God by means of the person and work of Jesus Christ, as prophesied in the Old Testament. The particular work of Christ that will be central to this gospel message is his death on the cross and resurrection from the dead. Second, we are given the *gospel mission* for which the apostles have been set apart (vv. 47–48). They are witnesses to the life, death, and resurrection of Christ. As such, they will proclaim his work, the required response of faith and repentance, and the benefit of the forgiveness of sins in his name. Third, we learn about the promised *gospel minister* who will empower the apostles as they fulfill their mission to proclaim the gospel in all nations (v. 49; see also Acts 1:8). The apostles have no inherent power in themselves to apply the gospel message as they engage in gospel mission. They must wait for the promised Holy Spirit to be poured out by Christ (Acts 1:8; 2:33), lest their proclamation of the Word fall like an empty sound upon spiritually deaf ears.

---

3 Romans 1:16–17; 3:21–26; 4:24–25; 5:1–2, 9–11, 12–17; 6:3–11; 8:1–4.

4 This name has often been ascribed to the book of Acts throughout history. The longer title is relevant here because the book serves as a detailed account of the apostles' actions following Christ's ascension, revealing how they understood the Great Commission.

THE APOSTLES' PRACTICE

The Great Commission passages did not just hang in midair, eluding definition. They meant something to the apostles, who were expected to immediately put them into practice. Our contention is that in the book of Acts we can see *how* the Holy Spirit illumined them to *practice* the doctrine they were taught. The apostolic *pattern of practice* is so consistent that it forms a model that is then commended to the church in every age.

It is not true that the church in every generation ought to imitate everything the apostles did in the book of Acts. The apostolic age is a unique and unrepeatable time in the history of God's story of salvation. The apostles are the foundation of the church who bore unique marks and a unique calling as the original eyewitnesses to the work of Christ (Luke 6:13; see also Acts 1:15–26; Eph 2:20; 2 Cor 12:12, Heb 2:4).[5] The apostles did not establish a succession of apostles but instead planted Scripture-saturated churches with elders and deacons (Acts 14:23; 20:17–35; 1 Tim 3:1–12; Titus 1:5–9).[6]

It is true, however, that the general pattern of practice of the apostles provides us with a reliable understanding of how the Holy Spirit illumined their minds to properly hear Jesus's teaching. We see a relentlessly consistent practice among the apostles as they engage in missionary work. In every instance, the evangelistic sermons of the apostles in Acts repeat the same pattern.[7] As Alan J. Thompson helpfully

---

5 It is not our task to address the question of the cessation or continuation of particular spiritual gifts. We are merely pointing to the generally accepted Protestant belief in the cessation of the office of apostle. The English Protestant confessions consistently held to the cessation of revelatory gifts (see 2LCF 1.1, WCF 1.1, Savoy Declaration 1.1). Likewise, John Calvin argued that those who hold to ongoing revelation are opponents of the Reformation (see John Calvin and Jacopo Sadoleto, *A Reformation Debate*, ed. John C. Olin [Grand Rapids: Baker, 1966]).

6 This Protestant understanding is contra Roman Catholicism's claims regarding the papacy. The only apostolic "succession" taught by the New Testament is the successive teaching of the apostolic message; see ch. 5 for a more detailed treatment of the issue.

7 See the appendix.

states, "These speeches, in keeping with Luke's practice of selectivity, are *typical* of more general accounts and thus we are to read these as *typical* of the way Paul would present the gospel to a synagogue audience and *typical* of the way he would present the gospel to a Gentile audience with no background knowledge of God's special revelation."[8]

Further, the apostles' sermons are abbreviated by Luke in a representative form with a repeated focus on the main elements of each sermon.[9] It is in this repeated practice of the apostles that the Holy Spirit teaches the church that "as in theology and ethics, so in preaching, we participate in *apostolic authority and power* by following *apostolic precept and example* as they are set forth in the pages of Scripture."[10]

THE GOSPEL MESSAGE

Jesus commanded the apostles to witness to his person and work as promised in accordance with the Scriptures (Luke 24:44–47, see also Matt 28:19). The apostles were so committed to the authority of the Scriptures that there is not an apostolic sermon that does not ground its argument in God's Word.[11] Thus, it is our task to look at the *content* of their gospel preaching. Further, we must consider the *consistent pattern* they followed in every evangelistic sermon and the *contextual accommodation* made for the sake of their hearers.

The content of the message of the apostles was consistently, and without exception, Jesus Christ and his work for the salvation of sinners. Jesus had told the apostles they would be his witnesses (Luke 24:48; Acts 1:8). They would testify to what they had seen and heard. They walked with him as he taught and performed miracles. They saw him falsely accused, tried, crucified, and buried. They found his empty

---

8   Alan J. Thompson, *The Acts of the Risen Lord Jesus: Luke's Account of God's Unfolding Plan*, ed. D. A. Carson, New Studies in Biblical Theology (Downers Grove, IL: InterVarsity Press, 2011), 27:89. Emphasis added.
9   Thompson, 27:89.
10 Roger Wagner, *Tongues Aflame: Learning to Preach from the Apostles* (Fearn, UK: Christian Focus, 2004), 31. Emphasis added.
11 We covered this commitment in ch. 1. We will look at it further in ch. 8.

tomb and rejoiced in his resurrection from the dead. They were with him for forty days as he opened the Scriptures and instructed them concerning the kingdom of God (Luke 24:44–49; Acts 1:3). The apostles knew their commission was to proclaim his death and resurrection while calling their listeners to respond in faith for the forgiveness of their sins (Luke 24:46–47; Acts 2:37–38; 16:30–31). This is the content of the gospel message they received and proclaimed in every single evangelistic sermon (1 Cor 15:1–11).[12]

The consistent pattern of the apostolic evangelistic sermons includes four essential components always provided in the same order.[13] First, the sermons always begin with God. Second, the sermons always speak of the person and work of Christ. Third, the sermons always call for the response of faith and repentance.[14] Fourth, the sermons always promise the benefits of forgiveness of sins and the reception of the Holy Spirit.[15]

The apostles also provide us a model of contextual accommodation in their approach to preaching the gospel message to various audiences. When the apostles preached to the Jews in Solomon's colonnade, they began with "the God of Abraham, the God of Isaac, and the God of Jacob" (Acts 3:13). Their audience knew the Old Testament. They were monotheists committed to the veracity of the Old Testament Scriptures and the worship of the God of their fathers. The apostles then preached Christ crucified and resurrected as the fulfillment of

---

12 See Greg Gilbert, *What Is the Gospel?* (Wheaton: Crossway, 2010) for a biblically thorough, helpful, and clear explanation of the content of the gospel.

13 Refer to the appendix for a chart that lays out these components for every evangelistic sermon in Acts.

14 Some sermons only require the response of repentance; others, faith; and some also include baptism and obedience. It is not our purpose here to provide an apologetic for faith in Christ as the sole instrument of justification. But we assume that the God-given faith that rests in Christ issues in the fruit of repentance and obedience and receives the sign of baptism. For more on this topic see John Murray, *Redemption Accomplished and Applied* (Grand Rapids: Eerdmans, 2015).

15 The gift of the Holy Spirit is also referred to as "times of refreshing" and "restoring all . . . things" (Acts 3:20–21), which is a reference to the promised restoration of Israel at the coming of the Holy Spirit in prophetic passages such as Isa 32:15 and Joel 2:28–32.

Old Testament promises with which the Jews were more than familiar (Acts 3:13–16). Further, the apostles called their Jewish audience to repentance and trust in Christ, which issued in benefits clothed in the language of the Jews' sacred writings (Acts 3:17–26).

But when the audience changed, the apostles accommodated their preaching of the content of the gospel to their new context. Peter's sermon to the God-fearing Gentile Cornelius began with God in a manner fitted to the question with which Cornelius was wrestling. Cornelius must have been wondering if the God of the Jews would show favor to a Gentile like himself. Thus, Peter's sermon began by introducing the "God [who] shows no partiality" (Acts 10:34). Peter then moved through the rest of his gospel content, making application to Cornelius. We see an even more dramatic example when Paul proclaimed the gospel message in Athens to pagan idolaters. They did not believe in one God who created all things or in a God who transcended creation. Thus, Paul began, "The God who made the world and everything in it, being Lord of heaven and earth, does not live in temples made by man, nor is he served by human hands, as though he needed anything, since he himself gives to all mankind life and breath and everything" (Acts 17:24–25).

The contextual accommodation of the apostolic evangelistic sermons assumes that the apostles knew their hearers' languages and worldviews. The apostles recognized that their hearers' errant theology must be understood, confronted, and corrected. Among certain peoples, they had to correct the doctrine of man, sin, and judgment to properly proclaim the saving message of the cross and resurrection of Jesus (Acts 17:26–31). Proclaiming Jesus as the answer to the problem of a people is not helpful if they have an improper understanding of God, man, and sin. In other words, Jesus is only the right answer if we are asking the right questions. Thus, contextual accommodation is never a work of changing the content of the message but rather of knowing language and culture well enough to correct the faulty understandings of concepts necessary to gospel proclamation. The apostles—and missionaries following in their example—are committed to this for the sake of guarding against syncretism.[16]

THE GOSPEL MISSION

The *gospel mission* of the apostles was to proclaim the *gospel message* in the power of the Holy Spirit to the nations as the means whereby Jesus would build his church.[17] Jesus is pleased to use the means of ordinary gospel preaching to achieve the goal of church planting. He commissioned his apostles to be gospel preachers (Luke 24:47). The apostles were commissioned as ambassadors of Christ to proclaim the gospel message and then to organize those who responded in faith into local churches.[18] Their mission was simple: preach the Word (2 Tim 4:1–2).

In our day, the primary methodology employed in missions to the unreached holds that we ought to gather unbelievers together and let them interpret the Scriptures on their own without the influence of outside teachers. One major proponent of this approach wrote to missionaries, "Do not teach or preach; instead, facilitate discovery and obedience. When people are simply exposed to the Scriptures, God will reveal the truth to them."[19] This kind of group-facilitated, self-discovery model has been praised as a fresh wind of the Holy Spirit ushering in church-planting movements in formerly difficult-to-reach places. The Christ-commissioned, Spirit-empowered model of gospel proclamation by the missionary is dismissed as traditional, Western, and ineffective.[20]

---

16 Syncretism is the blending of two different sets of beliefs, or religions, to create a third kind of religion. This is a prevalent problem in world missions and in our own local churches. We are always engaged in defending the church from blending biblical understandings of God and his work with our own cultural ideologies.
17 For more on the mission to the nations, see ch. 7.
18 For more on the church, see ch. 5.
19 Jerry Trousdale, *Miraculous Movements: How Hundreds of Thousands of Muslims are Falling in Love with Jesus* (Nashville: Thomas Nelson, 2012), 106.
20 See this article by a significant leader in modern missions: Ted Esler, "Coming to Terms: Two Church Planting Paradigms," *International Journal of Frontier Missiology* 30, no. 2 (Summer 2013) https://www.ijfm.org/PDFs_IJFM/30_2_PDFs/IJFM_30_2-Esler.pdf.

The apostolic mission clearly employed the *method* of gospel proclamation. In the book of Acts, "Verbs of teaching, proclaiming, refuting, reasoning and persuading require hearers to understand, think, reason, consider and examine."[21] It is true that the apostles are said to "dialogue" on occasion as they taught. Paul "reasoned" (*dielexato*) with the Jews in Thessalonica (Acts 17:2). But this verb "dialogue" is further explained with the two participles supplied by the next verse: "explaining" and "proving."[22] Additionally, the verse ends with Paul saying, "This Jesus, whom I proclaim to you, is the Christ" (Acts 17:3). Thus, even where the apostles are said to engage in dialogue, Luke is indicating that such dialogue is bold, authoritative teaching—not "self-discovery."

THE GOSPEL MINISTER

Finally, throughout the book of Acts, we are reminded of the only effectual minister, the Holy Spirit. On the night of his resurrection, Jesus commanded the apostles to wait in Jerusalem until he sent the promise of his Father upon them and they were clothed with power from on high (Luke 24:49). Just before his ascension, Jesus promised his apostles they would receive power when the Holy Spirit came upon them (Acts 1:8). When the Holy Spirit came upon the apostles, they began to proclaim the mighty works of God (Acts 2:11). The Holy Spirit was sent to empower Christ's church to boldly and effectively proclaim the gospel.[23] This Spirit-given "'boldness' is a freedom to proclaim the truth of God's saving purposes in the Lord Jesus along with the accompanying warnings and promises even in contexts of opposition, threats of personal harm, persecution or derision. It is the willingness 'to be clear in the face of fear.'"[24]

---

21 Thompson, *The Acts of the Risen Lord Jesus*, 27:93.
22 κατὰ δὲ τὸ εἰωθὸς τῷ Παύλῳ εἰσῆλθεν πρὸς αὐτοὺς καὶ ἐπὶ σάββατα τρία **διελέξατο** αὐτοῖς ἀπὸ τῶν γραφῶν, **διανοίγων** καὶ **παρατιθέμενος** ὅτι τὸν χριστὸν ἔδει παθεῖν καὶ ἀναστῆναι ἐκ νεκρῶν καὶ ὅτι οὗτός ἐστιν ὁ χριστὸς [ὁ] Ἰησοῦς ὃν ἐγὼ καταγγέλλω ὑμῖν.
23 Acts 2:29; 4:13, 29, 31; 9:27–28; 13:46; 14:3; 18:26; 19:8; 26:26; 28:31.
24 Thompson, *The Acts of the Risen Lord Jesus*, 97.

APPLICATION

The Holy Spirit is still at work today, empowering the church to boldly proclaim the gospel message.[25] The church sends forth missionary church planters to preach the gospel (Rom 10:14–15). The Holy Spirit empowers those preachers to speak boldly. He empowers their message to cut to the heart of God's people so that they look to Christ in faith. Missionaries are sent forth with the confidence that Christ has always worked powerfully by his Spirit and through his church in the same way. As the Protestant Reformer John Calvin said, "And forasmuch as Christ hath promised the same Spirit to all his servants, let us only defend the truth faithfully, and let us crave a mouth and wisdom of him, and we shall be sufficiently furnished to speak."[26]

STUDY QUESTIONS

1. Why do you suppose it is common to think doctrine is fixed by the Bible but methodology is neutral and undefined by Scripture?

2. What can we learn from the apostles regarding missionary methodology? Are we expected to repeat all the works we see among the apostles? What works are unique to them? In what ways is the contemporary church like them?

3. What was the content of the apostles' gospel proclamation? In what manner did they contextualize their gospel preaching to prevent syncretism? How do we guard against syncretism?

4. What was the consistent method in evangelism of the apostles? Are self-discovery Bible studies ever commended or modeled in Scripture as a method of evangelism?

---

25 For more on this, see ch. 4.
26 Quoted in Roger Wagner, *Tongues Aflame: Learning to Preach from the Apostles* (Fearn, UK: Christian Focus, 2004), 31.

5. What gifts has Christ given to his church for its upbuilding (Eph 4:7–16)? What concerns do the apostles have for Christ's church (Acts 20:28–31; 2 Tim 1:13–14; Titus 1:9–16)? What has Christ's church been known to do rather quickly (Gal 1:6–9)? How do these realities inform our missions methodology?

6. What are the implications of the apostles' method for the equipping of missionary church planters being sent to the nations? How do we prepare missionaries to clearly proclaim the gospel cross-culturally?

7

THE NATIONS AND THE CHURCH'S COMMISSION

Jesus Christ our Lord, through whom we have received grace and apostleship to bring about the obedience of faith for the sake of his name among all the nations.
Romans 1:4–5

Imagine emerging from the unpopulated jungles, thatched dwellings, and torrid air of the Pacific Islands into the lurid lights and blaring soundscapes of a concrete-clad U.S. metropolis—all to go and stand shoulder-to-shoulder in an arena with thousands of kempt American pastors.

Brooks Buser, now president of Radius International, attended a large evangelical gathering not long after giving a significant portion of his life serving the YembiYembi people of tropical Papua New Guinea. This would perhaps cause culture shock for anyone—but nothing like the culture shock Buser was to receive in a meeting with a young pastor during the event.

"What is your view of 'white privilege' and the 'social justice movement' and how they inform the Great Commission?" the pastor asked. Gently, Buser explained that these were not issues he had encountered while ministering to the unreached tribal people group. He then proceeded to challenge the young man to consider another form of privilege. Among the world's nearly 12,000 distinct ethnolinguistic people groups, more than 3,000 are completely without any significant witness to Jesus Christ.[1] This means there are at least 274 million people on the planet who, under the current circumstances, will likely never hear the gospel. This, Buser contended, constituted the greatest global disparity worthy of the church's labors.

Dismissively, yet with complete sincerity, the pastor responded, "You're not woke."

It is beyond the scope of this book to address the complex issues surrounding social justice and such concepts as "privilege" and "oppression" in the moral and political life of the West.[2] Injustice is real, and systems of law can be stained with sin. At the same time, secular ideologies aimed at addressing injustices are also marred by human depravity. The church is called to use both the gospel and God's law to influence the public sphere in the cause of righteousness. We believe the lordship of Christ has limitless implications for modern society. Yet this story reveals that our concern for "the nation" routinely eclipses our heart for *the nations*.

If we care about temporal injustices, we should care *more*—not less—about the eternal state of souls. As John Piper has remarked, "We care about all suffering now, especially eternal suffering later."[3] Yet as evangelicals increasingly fracture over matters of law and justice, we simultaneously tend to trivialize the missionary task—producing such slogans as "everyone is a missionary," redefining missions in terms of humanitarian relief, and allowing short-term missions to degenerate

---

[1] That is, people groups with a distinct, relatively contiguous self-identity involving a combination of ethnicity and language. More than three thousand ethnolinguistic people groups are considered unreached (consisting of less than 2 percent professing evangelical) and unengaged (lacking any known missionary outreach or biblically sound church-planting efforts). These definitions come from "People Groups," IMB Global Research 2020, accessed September 2, 2020, http://peoplegroups.org.

[2] For a detailed treatment of this subject, see Chad Vegas, "The Ultimate Injustice: Gospel Privilege and Global Missions," in Jared Longshore, ed., *By What Standard* (Cape Coral, FL: Founders, 2020), 137–151.

[3] John Piper, "Abortion and the Narrow Way That Leads to Life," *Desiring God*, January 23, 2011, https://www.desiringgod.org/messages/abortion-and-the-narrow-way-that-leads-to-life.

into a multimillion-dollar tourist industry.[4] Far too often, we ignore the greatest justice issue: the billions perishing under the wrath of God across the globe.

To possess the privilege of the gospel is to owe a debt to all the nations. As Paul remarked, "Woe to me if I do not preach the gospel!" (1 Cor 9:16). This is not a clever preacher's spin on the current political rhetoric but the very thread woven through Scripture's greatest treatise on the doctrine of salvation: the Epistle to the Romans.

THE MOST OVERLOOKED MISSIONARY SUPPORT LETTER

We are all familiar with how the apostle Paul ascends the heights of literary glory and plumbs the depths of doctrine throughout Romans—diagnosing the problem of sin (ch. 1–2), unfolding the wonders of the cross (3), defending justification by faith alone (4), contrasting the two humanities in Adam and Christ (5), working out the ethical implications of grace (6–7), charting out the life lived in the Spirit (8), and reveling in the doctrine of election (9–11). What we often miss, however, is that this same letter, in which Paul is so transfixed on the doctrine of salvation, is also a *missionary support letter*.

In Paul's introduction, we learn that he has "received grace and apostleship to bring about the obedience of faith for the sake of his name among all the nations" (Rom 1:5). The apostle concludes with a doxology to the God who is able to strengthen the Romans through the gospel that "has now been disclosed and through the prophetic writings has been made known to all nations, according to the command of the eternal God, to bring about the obedience of faith" (16:26). Note the recurring phrases "all the nations" and "obedience of faith," which form an *inclusio*, or bracketing effect, around the book. Paul further bookends the letter with the details of his traveling apostolic ministry to these nations. Paul wants to visit the church in Rome but has been

---

4 North Americans spend an estimated $3.1 billion on foreign short-term missions each year, according to Gilles Gravelle, "Short-Term Missions & Money," Moving Missions (2012), accessed September 7, 2020, movingmissions.org/wp-content/pdfs/short-term-missions-and-money.pdf.

hindered because of his unique calling to harvest more fruit from the Gentiles (1:10–13). And toward the letter's conclusion, Paul explains that he is writing the Roman church in part to solicit their support for his mission to Spain (15:23–29). When we read Romans as a missionary support letter, we see, in keeping with the thesis of this book, that robust theology begets mission, and mission is impossible without robust theology. From beginning to end, Romans is concerned with securing *the believing obedience of the nations*.

Central to Paul's message in Romans is his recognition of his *gospel privilege*. At the onset, we read, "I am under obligation both to Greeks and to barbarians, both to the wise and to the foolish" (1:14). I (Alex) once heard a pastor aptly summarize Paul's statement: "Those who *own* the gospel *owe* the gospel." Paul, seeing that he had the gospel message and others did not, recognized that he had a sacred duty to share his blessing with others who lacked it. The apostle looked out across the expanse of the Roman world and beyond and saw that he owed the Word of Christ to the civilized, the uncivilized, the Jew, and the pagan Gentile alike.

We can never repay our Lord for the free gift of grace, but we are expected to give him a return on his investment. This is a reality recognized even by unbelievers. Consider these candid remarks from noted atheist and entertainer Penn Jillette in 2010:

> If you believe that there is a heaven and hell, and people could be going to hell or not getting eternal life or whatever, and you think, "Well, it's not really worth telling them this because it would make it socially awkward,". . . how much do you have to hate somebody to not proselytize? How much do you have to hate somebody to believe that everlasting life is possible, and not tell them that? I mean, if I believed, beyond a shadow of a doubt, that a truck was coming at you, and you didn't believe it, . . . there's a certain point where I tackle you. And this is more important than that.[5]

---

5 Penn Jillette, "A Gift Of A Bible," YouTube, July 8, 2010, https://www.youtube.com/watch?v=6md638smQd8.

Whatever it means to be saved by grace apart from works, it does *not* mean that we are called into a life of comfortable ease or apathy. Believers who possess salvation must invest their lives in seeing others partake in that privilege.

Our purpose in this chapter is to biblically demonstrate (1) the obligation and (2) the strategy of the church to reach "all the nations" described in the Great Commission and in the words of Paul. Yet as we encounter God's heart for the nations in Romans, there are three potential ways in which we may interpret the apostle's words: (1) God is definitively accomplishing the salvation of every individual, (2) God is including all sorts of genuine seekers from among the nations in the saving benefits of Christ, or (3) God is calling out for himself a particular people from all the nations. We must take a brief detour and consider our choice between *universalism, inclusivism,* or *exclusivism.*

THE WAY FOR THE NATIONS

It is difficult to reflect honestly on the New Testament and overstate the depth of God's heart for the nations. God's electing love knows no national, cultural, linguistic, or geographic barriers. From the earliest unveiling of his redemptive plan to Abraham, God had in view all the nations of the earth (Gen 12:1–3). Later, he ordained Israel as a witness to the surrounding peoples (Deut 4:6–8; Psalm 67). This mission is accomplished in Christ. Jesus came to save the world (John 3:17). This must be contrasted with the pessimism that pervades much of contemporary evangelicalism, which holds that the world is spiraling toward disaster and that Christ will return to a church that has failed its mission. This cynicism does not comport with Jesus's promise to be present with us as we go into all the world (Matt 28:20). Not only is our Lord's mission global in scope but it is also *cosmic* in that he has purposed "to reconcile to himself all things, whether on earth or in heaven, making peace by the blood of his cross" (Col 1:20). Yet the vast scope of God's love does not make us immune from error. As we seek to embody God's heart for the world, we must guard against two twin errors that result from an imbalanced reading of Scripture: universalism and inclusivism.

Universalism is the belief that all religious paths lead to God and eternal life. This has become common in the West. "Christian universalism," or universal redemption, is the heretical belief that it is through Christ's redemptive work that *all will indeed be saved*. Origen of Alexandria, a third-century Christian scholar, is believed to have taken this view in his teaching on *apokatastasis*, the eventual restoration of all things to their original, unfallen state.

Universalism certainly satisfies a selfish impulse in our nature since it excises the unsavory doctrine of hell. The doctrine of hell is easier to live without. To embrace universalism is to absolve the Christian of any evangelistic responsibility. But Scripture does not give us this option. Both testaments loudly attest to the reality of eternal punishment (Isaiah 66; Luke 16:19–31; Revelation 20). One cannot read of torment, weeping, the gnashing of teeth, the undying worm, and a lake of fire and then conclude that hell is actually empty. This is not a matter open to debate among orthodox Christians. Whatever it means that Christ will save the nations, it cannot mean that all individuals are to be saved.

Whereas universalism posits that all *will* be saved, inclusivism posits that all *may* be saved. Inclusivists affirm the uniqueness of Christ but deny that faith in him is the only way to receive his saving benefits. Sincere adherents to other religions may be included in Christ. Thus, a faithful Buddhist or devout Muslim could be saved, unbeknownst to him, through Christ—even if such persons explicitly *denied* Christ in life.

Inclusivism involves a more subtle form of error than universalism since it seems to go further than universalism in affirming the uniqueness of Christ. Yet Scripture is clear here as well. In the New Testament we read again and again not only that Jesus is the unique Savior but also that his saving benefits must be through faith alone (John 3:36; 8:24; Rom 10:9–15; Heb 11:6). While we may find some good in the religious traditions of the world, Scripture will not allow us to conclude that these graces are saving graces. Indeed, "the gate is narrow and the way is hard that leads to life, and those who find it are few" (Matt 7:14).

Over against both universalism and inclusivism, the Bible teaches the global scope of God's redemptive purposes as well as the exclusivity of Christ. Jesus taught that if one is not for him, one is against him (Matt 12:30). Before his death, he told his disciples that he was the only way to the Father (John 14:6)—not merely meaning that all the world's religions ultimately route through him but that one can only come to God through faith in the Son. The apostles, who walked with Jesus for years and heard his direct teaching, testified that "there is salvation in no one else, for there is no other name under heaven given among men by which we must be saved" (Acts 4:12). It is necessary that we relate to Jesus directly and personally (hence "no other name") to enjoy his saving benefits. Because Christ is the perfect image of God, one who rejects Christ rejects God (1 John 2:23). Though faith in Jesus Christ is incredibly *inclusive* in that all nations are invited to repent and believe, it is also *exclusive* because God only saves those who believe in Christ. No other religion is capable of uniting a sinner to the perfect redemptive work of the incarnate God-man.

The exclusivity of Christ lays great responsibility on the people of God to reach the nations with his good news. This is Paul's logic in Romans 10. After explaining that "everyone who calls on the name of the Lord will be saved" (v. 13), he is quick to draw out the missionary imperative: "How then will they call on him in whom they have not believed? And how are they to believe in him of whom they have never heard? And how are they to hear without someone preaching? And how are they to preach unless they are sent? As it is written, 'How beautiful are the feet of those who preach the good news!'" (vv. 14–15).

If we confess the exclusivity of Christ, our faith demands boot leather! In keeping with the missionary thrust of Romans from chapter 1, Paul explains that Christ secures the obedience of nations through the missionary obedience of the church. But who are these nations?

WHO ARE "THE NATIONS"?

In the Great Commission, Jesus gave his apostles—and us, by extension—the task to "go therefore and make disciples of all nations [*panta ta ethne*], baptizing them in the name of the Father and of the Son and of the Holy Spirit, teaching them to observe all that I have commanded you" (Matt 28:19–20). On its face, the question "Who are the nations?" may seem unnecessary. Is it not enough that God has commanded us to go into all the world? Why split hairs? Yet our answer to this question has the potential to drastically reshape the missionary enterprise.

Individuals?

Did our Lord simply intend his followers to evangelize the largest number of individuals? There is an undeniable element of truth in this interpretation. God does not delight in the death of the wicked (Ezek 18:23). God desires the salvation of all kinds of people (1 Tim 2:4) and is not willing that any of his people should perish (2 Pet 3:9). What a merciful God we serve!

Yet to stop here in our analysis would not capture the nuance of Jesus's words or the way in which the apostles applied them. The parable of the lost sheep (Matt 18:12–13) reminds us that the Lord is not simply concerned with amassing the largest number of converts possible. In Acts, the Holy Spirit directed Paul away from Asia Minor (16:6), where there was a preponderance of lost souls. At the book's conclusion, Paul appears to give up on evangelizing the Jews in Rome altogether (28:25–28). In Romans 9, we see that God receives more glory in choosing some for salvation (but not others) than he would if he equally intended all to be saved (vv. 18–24). And in Romans 15, a passage to which we will return, Paul even says that his apostolic job was "done" from Jerusalem to Illyricum (vv. 19, 23)—an impossible claim if the missionary task is conceived merely in terms of total converts. If God's goal is simply to save as many individuals as possible, these passages make little sense. Jesus, by saying "go and make disciples of all nations," meant more than that we should seek to convert the largest possible number of individuals.

Nation-States?

What if we think of the Great Commission in terms of reaching countries or lands? This interpretation also has warrant. Jesus describes the apostles' witness as extending from Jerusalem and Judea to Samaria and the ends of the earth (Acts 1:8; see also Ps 22:27). Other texts remind us that the knowledge of the Lord will spread over all the earth (Isa 11:9; Hab 2:14). It is natural to conceive of the spread of the gospel in geographic terms. Yet this does not exhaust the purpose of the Great Commission.

Church history shows that a geographic conception of the kingdom of God has often been conflated with political ends, with dubious results. When the Roman Empire receded, medieval Roman Catholicism filled the void. Emerging from the Protestant Reformation, the Western church struggled to break free from this geopolitical conception of Christendom. Prominent evangelical missiologist Ralph Winter saw the modern missions movement (beginning with William Carey in the nineteenth century) split into multiple eras—the first two focusing, respectively, on reaching continental coastlands and inland provinces.[6] Yet a purely geographic conception of the church's mission stops short of our Lord's intention. If Christ only intended that Christian witness should be present in each of the world's two hundred sovereign countries, then our mission would be virtually complete already.

Ethnolinguistic People Groups?

In the 1970s, missiologists Ralph Winter and Donald McGavran put forward the concept of "hidden peoples"—those not easily reached by traditional evangelistic efforts—which developed into the now more

---

6 See Ralph Winter, "Three Mission Eras and the Loss and Recovery of Kingdom Mission, 1800–2000," *Perspectives on the World Christian Movement: A Reader, Fourth Edition* (Wiliam Carey Library, 2013), 263–278.

well-known concept of "unreached people groups."[7] These missiologists defined the *ethne* of the Great Commission as *ethnolinguistic people groups*—"distinguished by [their] self-identity with traditions of common descent, history, customs and language."[8] The missionary task, they asserted, was to reach these groups by ensuring that there was a sufficient baseline of Christian witness available and present in a given language and cultural context to enable the successful evangelization of that group to unfold.

Recognizing distinct people groups within a broader society matters because evangelistic efforts do not tend to blanket any society uniformly. Two people groups may inhabit the same borders, but to bring the gospel from one to the other may involve significant cross-cultural and cross-linguistic work. Or it may be that believers among the majority people group (such as the Han Chinese) are unable or unwilling to associate with a minority people group (such as the Uyghur Muslims in China). We must, then, pay attention to which people groups themselves have access to the gospel within their own language and cultural setting. A widely accepted definition of a "reached" people group is one with more than 2 percent professing evangelical in its population and more than 5 percent nominal Christian; anything below this threshold is considered "unreached."[9]

Defining the "nations" this way is largely consistent with the biblical witness. God is interested in the worship of every tribe, tongue, people, and nation (Rev 5:9). Christ, the seed of Abraham, was to bless

---

7 Winter defined these hidden peoples as "any linguistic, cultural or sociological group defined in terms of its primary affinity (not secondary or trivial affinities), which cannot be won by E-1 methods [that is, standard evangelistic methods not involving translation or bridging from one cultural group to another] and drawn into an existing fellowship of believers." Winter, "Unreached Peoples: The Development of the Concept," *International Journal of Frontier Missions* 1, no. 2 (1984): 131.
8 Ralph D. Winter and Bruce A. Koch, "Finishing the Task: The Unreached Peoples Challenge," *Perspectives on the World Christian Movement: A Reader, Fourth Edition* (William Carey Library, 2013), 534.
9 This threshold, though somewhat arbitrary, represents the supposed point at which a Christian movement within a population is reasonably able to evangelize the whole.

all the families of the earth (Gen 12:3). God is seeking to redeem not just people in general but *peoples* as sociological or cultural units. These distinct peoples do not fit neatly into the political borders we draw around nation-states but must be understood in their natural groupings according to language, heritage, and culture. We see an example of this sort of thinking in Acts: "Now those who were scattered because of the persecution that arose over Stephen traveled as far as Phoenicia and Cyprus and Antioch, speaking the word to no one except Jews. But there were some of them, men of Cyprus and Cyrene, who on coming to Antioch spoke to the Hellenists also, preaching the Lord Jesus" (11:19–20).

Hellenists (Greeks, or Greek-speaking Jews specifically) and the more traditional Aramaic-speaking Jews represented two distinct people groups in the first-century world. The believers from Cyprus and Cyrene are commended for reaching both of them, bringing the gospel across a cultural divide. Our Lord wants to see each people group evangelized, discipled, and assimilated into his body.

The ethnolinguistic definition is not without pitfalls, however. First, it is dangerous to load Scripture with modern sociological freight. We cannot assume that when Jesus commissioned his followers to disciple the *ethne*, he had in mind the precise number of 17,439 ethnolinguistic people groups as set by some modern researchers.[10] Such precision is often illusory.[11] Many of these people groups have arisen and gone extinct in the ages both before and after our Savior's parting words. Another danger is in assuming we can complete the task of missions simply by attaining a base minimum level of conversions in each people group, thereby ushering in the Lord's return. To reason in this way

---

10   This figure is used by Joshua Project, a ministry of Frontier Ventures (formerly the U.S. Center for World Mission) in Pasadena, CA (founded by the late Ralph Winter). See "Joshua Project," Joshua Project, Frontier Ventures, accessed January 2, 2021, https://joshuaproject.net.

11   As a case in point regarding such imprecision, the figure listed was 17,441 when this chapter was initially drafted and was downwardly revised while this chapter was undergoing editing. This should not be taken as a wholesale rejection of the use of statistics in missiology; rather, it should give us pause if we are inclined to think we can perfectly quantify the Great Commission using human instrumentation.

is to deny our Lord his sovereign prerogative to determine the spread, timing, and consummation of his kingdom. Our task is not to generate a minimum number of converts but to fully *disciple* the nations (Matt 28:19), a task that is ongoing. A final danger is that we base our strategy exclusively on such externals as ethnicity or race, forgetting that God looks on the heart rather than the outward appearance (1 Sam 16:7). We must not commit the sin of partiality in our missiology (Jas 2:1). Still, there is much we can learn from the ethnolinguistic approach definition.

Gentiles in General?

It is important for us to define "the nations" biblically before we define it sociologically. A compelling case can be made that "the nations" in the Great Commission refers to any and all Gentiles indiscriminately.[12] Recall that, formerly, the human race had been a single people until God divided the peoples at the tower of Babel (Genesis 11).[13] From the famed table of nations in the book of Genesis come the Gentile nations we encounter throughout biblical history. Yet God set apart Abraham's lineage to be a "great nation" (Gen 12:2) in distinction to the other dispersed peoples. It was these nations to whom Israel's worship was to be a witness (Mark 11:17) and from whom God would one day gather his elect people (Isa 66:12, 18–20). Thus, for the Jewish readers of Matthew's Gospel—indeed, for the apostles themselves—to speak of the "nations" was not merely to refer to particular ethnic or cultural units but to make a statement concerning those who were not of Israel, strangers to the covenant, and pagan (Rom 2:14–15; Eph 2:11–12). In sending his disciples to the nations, Jesus was not making

---

12 This is argued by Darren Carlson and Elliot Clark, "The 3 Words That Changed Missions Strategy—and Why We Might Be Wrong," The Gospel Coalition, September 11, 2019, https://www.thegospelcoalition.org/article/misleading-words-missions-strategy-unreached-people-groups.

13 Deut 32:8 editorializes the Babel incident as follows: "When the Most High gave to the nations their inheritance, when he divided mankind, he fixed the borders of the peoples according to the number of the sons of God." Note that the Septuagint translates the Hebrew term for "nations" (*goyim*) with the same word *ethne* that appears in the calling of Abraham (Gen 12:2) and the Great Commission.

a statement about anthropology but was indicating the removal of the covenantal barrier between Jew and Gentile. The apostles were eventually obedient to this commission, and the gospel was proclaimed to "all nations" in the first century (Col 1:23; 1 Tim 3:16)—that is, to all sorts of peoples in the known world. Today, the gospel of free grace in Christ must be preached indiscriminately to all Jews and Gentiles, and we should not spend more time identifying the nations than reaching them.

It is undeniable that a major thrust of the Great Commission and of Paul's use of "the nations" in Romans has to do with the extension of the kingdom to non-Jews in addition to Jews. But "all nations without distinction" does not exhaust the meaning of *panta ta ethne*. To make disciples of "all" the nations, we reach both *any* nation (all without distinction) and *every* nation (all without exception). To accomplish the latter and reach every nation, we must know what a nation is. In other words, to say that "all the nations" means "Jews and Gentiles in general" does not help us define a nation as a unit. Only by defining a nation as a unit can we understand how to go about evangelizing and discipling a nation.

LANGUAGE GROUPS

The best approach is to combine sensitivity to the biblical-theological definition with the best of current missiological insight. We can recognize the covenantal implications of Jesus's commission to the Gentiles without becoming blind to the distinctions between people groups that inhibit ordinary evangelism. We can also recognize the distinctness of each *ethne* without losing our sense of wonder at the fact that Gentiles are now included in God's kingdom.

Arguably, no defining mark of a people group matters more to the missionary than language. Only when the gospel is preached in all the languages of the nations can we begin to think that the global church has approached the completion of our Lord's command. Only the Lord knows when the Great Commission will have been fulfilled from the divine standpoint. Yet the greatest practical consideration that can drive the church is that we would make the gospel equally accessible in all the languages spoken by the distinct peoples of the world. Thus, it is most helpful for missions strategists to speak of peoples and nations in terms of *language groups*.

As with many biblical keywords, the definition of "nation" varies in nuance according to context. Yet Jesus's orders to his people concerning the nations are astonishingly unambiguous. The people of Christ are called to evangelize and disciple every people. This is because Christ is building his church among all peoples. Consider how the apostle John draws back the veil of eternity in Revelation 5:9–10: "And they [the twenty-four elders] sang a new song, saying, 'Worthy are you to take the scroll and to open its seals, for you were slain, and by your blood you ransomed people for God from every tribe and language and people and nation, and you have made them a kingdom and priests to our God, and they shall reign on the earth.'"

Christ has purchased an elect people drawn from among the nations, and the church is the means by which our Lord accomplishes the evangelization and salvation of this people. But no single believer or local church can do this alone. Journeying on through Romans, we must ask: How did Paul envision this task being accomplished?

FULFILLING THE MINISTRY OF THE GOSPEL

As Paul winds down his treatise, he returns to the occasion for his writing in Romans 15. If we study Paul's logic, we will discover his strategy for how the church is to reach all the *ethne* (Gentiles, or nations; Rom 15:16):

> In Christ Jesus, then, I have reason to be proud of my work for God. For I will not venture to speak of anything except what Christ has accomplished through me to bring the Gentiles to obedience—by word and deed, by the power of signs and wonders, by the power of the Spirit of God—so that from Jerusalem and all the way around to Illyricum *I have fulfilled the ministry of the gospel of Christ*; and

thus I make it my ambition to preach the gospel, not where Christ has already been named, lest I build on someone else's foundation, but as it is written, "Those who have never been told of him will see, and those who have never heard will understand." (vv. 17–21, emphasis added)

With a sound conscience, Paul says he has "fulfilled" his gospel ministry from Jerusalem to Illyricum (an area of Eastern Europe near the Balkan Peninsula's Adriatic coast). How can this be? Surely Paul had not personally evangelized the entire population between these two major centers. Millions remained lost.

The answer comes in the following verses. Paul sought to preach where a "foundation" had not yet been laid (v. 20). We can infer that his ministry from Jerusalem to Illyricum was one of foundation-laying. Luke's outline of Paul's earlier ministry supports this conclusion:

1. Paul "preached the gospel to that city and had made many disciples" (Acts 14:21).
2. He "returned . . . strengthening the souls of the disciples, encouraging them to continue in the faith" (vv. 21–22).
3. He finally "appointed elders for them in every church, with prayer and fasting they committed them to the Lord in whom they had believed" (v. 23).

Paul's goal was not to exhaustively evangelize an entire population. His task was to preach the gospel and gather disciples into local church bodies with qualified eldership. Each church was intended as an outpost for continued evangelization. As an apostle, Paul was the pioneer; the disciples he left behind were responsible for saturating their communities with the gospel.

There is much important ministry work to be done on existing foundations, in places where churches are established. Evangelism, church planting, biblical counseling, teaching, and mercy ministry must continue in these contexts. But with Paul, the church of Jesus Christ must also devote focused attention to "those who have never heard" (Rom 15:21). Our hearts should break particularly for those nations among whom

Christ has not yet been named. Only once we embrace Paul's holy ambition can we reasonably envision a day in which all the distinct peoples and language groups are brought to the obedience of faith.

APPLICATION

It is inexcusable that those who most cherish the theology of Romans have at times most failed to recognize its missionary implications. William Carey and Andrew Fuller both belonged to the English Calvinistic Baptist stream of tradition of the eighteenth century that had a high regard for the doctrines of grace. Yet both fought some of their fiercest theological battles against men of their own tribe who were convinced that divine election rendered the Great Commission obsolete. They, like far too many in our day, knew the doctrines of grace but forgot the grace of those doctrines.[14] Our gospel privilege obliges us to men and women of all nations. We owe every country, culture, and language the same access to the gospel we enjoy. This gracious weight laid on us drives us to action in three ways.

First, the church is obliged to send missionaries to all people groups. In contrast with the apathy of the British hyper-Calvinists of Carey and Fuller's day, consider the way in which the Synod of Dort—a landmark council in the seventeenth century defining the Reformed doctrine of salvation—derived the missionary imperative from its theology of election: "It is the promise of the gospel that whoever believes in Christ crucified shall not perish but have eternal life. This promise, together with the command to repent and believe, ought to be announced and declared without differentiation or discrimination to all nations and people, to whom God in his good pleasure sends the gospel."[15]

We must feel the weight of this "ought." The free grace offered in the gospel demands to be freely offered to all nations and people. We

---

14 This phrase borrowed from Sinclair Ferguson, "What Jonah Learned" (Philadelphia Conference on Reformed Theology, Philadelphia, PA, 2006).
15 The Synod of Dort (1618–1619), *The Canons of Dort* (Pensacola: Chapel Library, 2010), 2.5, https://www.chapellibrary.org:8443/pdf/books/codo.pdf.

should be zealous, as was the Synod of Dort, to protect the purity of our doctrine. But this must never come at the expense of our zeal for the nations to know Christ.

Second, the church is *particularly* obligated to those nations among whom no gospel foundation has been laid. It is true that the gospel should be declared to all nations without discrimination, but it is also true that we must discern whether we have in fact excluded any nations from hearing. In our case, we have. According to some counts, there are as many as 78,000 evangelical Christians—or 900 churches—for every unreached ethno-linguistic people group. Approximately 95 percent of the world's 4.19 million Christian workers work within the Christianized world, broadly speaking. And in 2001, only about 1 percent of giving to "missions" in general went to the unreached.[16] The problem is cyclical; these peoples will remain least-reached as long as they are overlooked by funds and workers. If we care about justice and equity, these disparities should haunt us.

This means that we must prayerfully mobilize both Pauline-type and Timothean-type missionaries. By "Pauline," we refer to those missionaries who, with Paul, make it their ambition to preach Christ where he is not yet known. With the term "Timothean," we have in view those who, like Timothy, are left behind or sent into a new context to strengthen an existing ministry or body of believers (see 1 Tim 1:3). Currently, the number of Timothy-style missionaries sent from North American churches is disproportionately large in light of the colossal number of unreached peoples. It is perhaps true that trailblazing, pioneering, Paul-style gospel workers will always be a minority in short supply. The Spirit of God is sovereign over the gifts he gives to his church (1 Cor 12:11). But we must also preach to and disciple believers in such a way as would cause more of them to embrace a Pauline-like vocation. We must teach ourselves and others to expect suffering, embrace risk, and care for those without gospel access. Most

---

16 "Missions Stats: The Current State of the World," The Traveling Team, accessed September 19, 2020, http://www.thetravelingteam.org/stats.

of all, we are to petition the Lord earnestly to raise up more such laborers (Matt 9:38; Luke 10:2). Perhaps we have not because we ask not.

Finally, the church and its workers must prioritize culture and language acquisition. We cannot content ourselves to let the gospel reside only with a few nations or cultures we already understand. Neither should we sit idly by while the Western church enjoys a preponderance of theological resources, education, and training while indigenous believers in the Majority World suffer the savage effects of false teaching. Biblically informed, theologically versed mission workers must give themselves to understanding language, culture, and tradition so as to bring the whole counsel of God's Word to bear on fledgling local churches across the globe. We must employ *means* to get the gospel from one people to the next. Otherwise, our claim that the gospel is for all nations will ring hollow. J. Gresham Machen, the founder of Westminster Theological Seminary, aptly summarized this great responsibility of the church:

> It may be said simply that the Christian way of salvation is narrow only so long as the Church chooses to let it remain narrow. The name of Jesus is discovered to be strangely adapted to men of every race and of every kind of previous education. And the Church has ample means, with promise of God's Spirit, to bring the name of Jesus to all. If, therefore, this way of salvation is not offered to all, it is not the fault of the way of salvation itself, but the fault of those who fail to use the means that God has placed in their hands.[17]

We conclude this chapter as we began. Brooks Buser's father, Brad Buser, is also a missionary who spent more than two decades pouring out his life among the formerly cannibalistic Iteri people of Papua New Guinea. Brad, his wife, his daughter, and his three sons endured the loss of bodily comforts and the privileges of a typical American lifestyle. In one conversation, he related that what sustained him was the joy of standing before the Lord and saying, "Here is the Iteri church; here is how my life was spent. Here is the YembiYembi church; . . .

---

17 J. Gresham Machen, *Christianity and Liberalism* (Grand Rapids: Eerdmans, 1923), 124.

here is how the life of my boys was spent."[18] Our Lord has purchased the nations with his blood and sent us to them. May our cry be that of the Moravian missionaries: "May the Lamb that was slain receive the reward of his suffering!"

STUDY QUESTIONS

1. In what sense is the great global disparity in access to the gospel message an "injustice" demanding our attention?
2. Why is it not legalistic or works-righteous to say that the believer in Christ owes a debt to the unbelieving world?
3. In what sense is the gospel invitation an inclusive message? In what sense is the gospel an exclusive message?
4. What would Jesus's hearers have understood him to be saying when he commissioned them to "the nations"? How should we define "the nations" today?
5. How did the apostle Paul "fulfill" his gospel ministry across the ancient world? How can we reach all the nations today?
6. What can missionaries today do to focus on making the gospel as widely available as possible to the world's peoples?

---

18 This occurred in a private conversation between Brad Buser and Chad Vegas.

8

THE POWER OF ORDINARY GOSPEL PREACHING

*But we have this treasure in jars of clay, to show that the
surpassing power belongs to God and not to us.*
2 Corinthians 4:7

When I (Chad) was a younger man considering the prospect of planting a church, I asked for a meeting with a man who had spent the greater part of his life as a church-growth consultant. His name was Bob Brady. He was a godly man and a member of the megachurch where I served as a youth pastor. Bob had helped the church where I served become a "seeker-sensitive" church. He taught us how to reach the community with enormous success, just he had helped numerous other churches experience similar success. Yet, when I heard he had gone through a personal theological reformation and had repented of much of his life's work, I was startled and had to ask why. Bob had come to the conclusion that his understanding of ministry methodology was unfaithful to the Word of God. He summarily repented and wrote to every church he had consulted offering to help undo the unbiblical methods he had taught them.

As I sat with a couple of members of my church-planting team at Bob's kitchen table, I asked him about the church-growth movement and church planting. I will never forget that providential lunch. Bob reviewed the early part of his career when he was surveying the fastest growing churches in America to figure out the common ingredients of growing churches. He told us a story that startled him as a young church-growth consultant. Grace Community Church in Sun Valley, California, was one of the fastest growing churches in America when he went to study their ministry. Bob sat with his team at a table with the pastor, Dr. John MacArthur. Bob recalled asking why Dr. MacArthur believed the church was growing so rapidly. He said that Dr. MacArthur replied sharply, "It isn't the punch and cookies." He said that Dr. MacArthur looked straight at the team and pounded the table with his fist as he repeated three times, "Preach the Word! Preach the Word! Preach the Word!" Bob's team left the meeting smugly confident that Dr. MacArthur was too naïve to know why his church had experienced such dramatic growth. Bob then looked directly at me and said, "Chad, I was wrong. I did not understand biblical ministry. If you are going to plant a church, then I have only one admonition for you: Preach the Word! Preach the Word! Preach the Word!"

This lesson in church planting in my own language and culture has direct application to church planting in a foreign language and culture. We must eschew the unbiblical error that ministry here and missions abroad are *essentially* different tasks. Yes, there are differences in *circumstances* between ministry here and abroad.[1] But there are no differences in *essence*. Wherever we send missionaries, the nature of God, man, sin, Christ, and ministry do not change. The missionary work of the Holy Spirit in which he witnesses to Christ through the church remains the same. Language, culture, government, economics, climate, topography, architecture, and religious and ethnic heritage are all varied circumstances in which we will contextualize our ministry while retaining the same essential task. The power in ministry here and missions abroad is found, by the ordination of God, in gospel preaching alone.

It is true that systematic and patient preaching and teaching on the mission field can seem like ineffective, slow, and plodding work filled with sacrifice, suffering, and loss. From a human perspective, this method seems too ordinary and feeble. It appears ineffective and

---

1 2LCF 1.6. See also WCF 1.6.

unnecessary to exercise a method wherein one spends years learning language and culture, living in difficult contexts and suffering, only to spend several more years slowly and systematically proclaiming the gospel, planting churches, and teaching people toward maturity. Where is the rapid multiplication of church-planting movements? How is this method going to catalyze disciple-making movements? Isn't this traditional understanding of ministry methodology just quenching the new and fresh work of the Holy Spirit? Shouldn't we be more expectant of the Holy Spirit to powerfully bring about an extraordinary revival? Isn't God able to do wondrously and exceedingly beyond all we can ask or think?

God is able to do whatever God decrees. As stated in a previous chapter, the question is not, What is God able to do? God can make stones cry out and donkeys speak. The question is, What has God given his church to do? God has commanded his church to proclaim the gospel of Jesus Christ in the power of the Holy Spirit. This is ordinary work. This is long-suffering work. This is foolish work in the eyes of the world. The Holy Spirit can breathe forth a revival whenever he is pleased to do so, but the work of the church remains the same.

We have already surveyed the overall approach of the apostles throughout the book of Acts in implementing Christ's command to make disciples of all nations. Now we narrow our focus. It is our contention that a proper understanding of the biblical gospel necessitates a ministry methodology understood, employed, and taught by the apostle Paul. Paul understood that the very nature of the gospel required a ministry method that relied on the power of God alone in the proclamation of Christ alone.[2] He knew he was given the ordinary means of gospel preaching to accomplish his missionary call to make Christ known to the nations. Paul was committed to the belief that the Spirit of God would work supernaturally as he preached Christ (1 Cor 2:1–5). The

---

2 Paul's ministry was accompanied with signs and wonders confirming his apostolic office (2 Cor 12:12), yet he believed it was the Holy Spirit working through the proclamation of the gospel that caused the new birth and imparted the gift of faith (Rom 1:16; 1 Cor 2:1–5; 2 Cor 4:1–6; Eph 2:1–9).

Spirit may be pleased to use his work for the salvation or the condemnation of his hearers (2 Cor 2:14–17).

Paul had no control over outcomes in his missionary work. His sole responsibility was to proclaim Christ. Paul was ridiculed for his commitment to this ordinary means of gospel preaching. His preaching was not drawing the crowds, the financial resources, or the accolades being seen by the so-called super-apostles (2 Cor 10:10–12; 11:12–15). Paul was content to reply that he boasts not in his strength but in his weakness (11:30–12:11). He understood that the surpassing power in gospel ministry belongs only to God (4:7–12). Thus, Paul repudiated the use of any means that located the power for ministry in himself. He believed that to employ any worldly inventions to improve on the ordinary means of gospel proclamation is to empty the cross of its power and cause men to rest their faith on something other than the power of God (1 Cor 1:17; 2:5).

Our project in this chapter is to look more closely at the missionary's commitment to ordinary gospel proclamation and the true obstacle to, the central focus of, and the power in his ordinary gospel proclamation.

Paul's Commitment to Ordinary Gospel Proclamation

In the face of challenges from the Corinthian church, which criticized him for being unattractive, rhetorically weak, and evangelistically ineffective when compared with the super-apostles, Paul repeatedly returned to his commitment to his ordinary method: "Therefore, having this ministry by the mercy of God, we do not lose heart. But we have renounced disgraceful, underhanded ways. We refuse to practice cunning or to tamper with God's word, but by the open statement of the truth we would commend ourselves to everyone's conscience in the sight of God" (2 Cor 4:1–2).

Paul knew that he received his missionary calling by the electing love of the Father, the purchased grace of the Son, and the applicatory work of the Holy Spirit (Eph 1:3–14; Gal 1:11–16). His missionary call was a new covenant ministry of righteousness and life by the powerful working of the Holy Spirit (2 Cor 3:6–9). The nature of his missionary call meant he was personally insufficient; thus, his confidence had to be found in God alone (2 Cor 2:16; 3:4–6).

For God to ordain that his holy and gracious Son, our Lord Jesus Christ, would be known by the proclamation of our unclean lips could be nothing other than mercy to us. If the proclamation of the gospel were dependent on the rhetorical articulation of our lips, the mental prowess of our minds, or the purity of love from our hearts, the peoples would undoubtedly be lost and without hope. But because the missionary has been given this ministry by the mercy of God, there is no reason to lose heart. This emboldens the missionary to renounce human inventions and additions to the ordinary means God has given. The missionary may hear of those who boast of great power in ministry through their cunning new measures yet remain steadfastly opposed to tampering with God's Word.

It is essential for the missionary to note that sacred writ teaches us to repudiate worldly methods and embrace God-ordained methods. It is a basic assumption among many in missions circles that methods are neutral. Paul did not share this sentiment. He was committed to renouncing methods he believed were not commended by God. Paul repudiated those who employed the means of entertainment and soaring rhetoric (1 Cor 1:17; 2:1–5). He refused to be like those who watered down the gospel to sell it to larger crowds (2 Cor 2:17). He refused to do anything that would conceal the whole truth of Christianity in an effort to make himself or the gospel look more attractive. The eighteenth-century Baptist pastor and theologian John Gill wrote the following:

> They abhorred and rejected everything that was scandalous and reproachful to the Gospel of Christ; in simplicity and godly sincerity, not with fleshly wisdom, but by the grace of God, they had their conversation in the world; they were open and above board, both in principle and practice; the same men in public, as in private; they used no art to cover their doctrines, or hide their conversations;

everything of this kind was detestable to them. . . . They used no sly and artful methods to please men, to gain applause from them, or make merchandise of them; they did not lie in wait to deceive, watching an opportunity to work upon credulous and incautious minds; they did not, by good words and fair speeches, deceive the hearts of the simple; nor put on different forms, or make different appearances, in order to suit themselves to the different tempers and tastes of men. . . . They did not corrupt [the Word of God] with human doctrines, or mix and blend it with philosophy, and vain deceit; they did not wrest the Scriptures to serve any carnal or worldly purpose; nor did they accommodate them to the lusts and passions of men; or conceal any part of truth, or keep back anything which might be profitable to the churches.[3]

Paul repudiated any method that attempted to make Christianity more attractive or less offensive to unbelievers. He rejected any method that attempted to reach unbelievers by any means other than "by the open statement of the truth" (2 Cor 4:2). The super-apostles were hucksters. They were pragmatists. They did whatever worked in gathering a crowd. Paul was committed to openly and clearly proclaiming the whole unvarnished truth (Col 4:3–4). He did not occlude the difficult doctrines to avoid being persecuted and disparaged by men. He knew the world found his gospel foolish. He embraced the suffering, rejection, and ridicule that would come from preaching Christ. The truly humble minister openly declares the truth of the Word of God with no regard for the approval of man (Gal 1:6–10). He is the minister who knows this gospel may be foolish to the world but that it is the power of God for those who are being saved (1 Cor 1:18).

THE OBSTACLE TO ORDINARY GOSPEL PROCLAMATION

Paul could confidently rest in the ordinary means God had given because he did not have a false estimation of the true obstacle to his gospel ministry. He knew that the true obstacle to his missionary work of gospel proclamation was found not in the ordinary means of gospel

---

[3] John Gill, *An Exposition of the New Testament*, The Baptist Commentary Series (London: Mathews and Leigh, 1809), 2:777.

preaching but in the hearers themselves: "And even if our gospel is veiled, it is veiled to those who are perishing. In their case the god of this world has blinded the minds of the unbelievers, to keep them from seeing the light of the gospel of the glory of Christ, who is the image of God" (2 Cor 4:3–4).

Paul's gospel proclamation never offended his hearers due to his lack of personal charisma or rhetorical power but because the gospel always falls flat on the ears of those who are constitutionally deaf and perishing (Rom 11:7–8). They did not see Christ placarded before them in the preaching of the gospel because their eyes were blinded by the god of this world. The ultimate problem lies neither in the message nor the messenger but in those to whom the message is proclaimed. Just because men love the darkness does not thereby mean that the light is impure.

Therefore, it is not the role of the missionary to find a means of ministry that is more suitable to men of darkened minds and hardened hearts. The missionary has no power in himself to overcome the ultimate problem of his hearer. We cannot arrange our ministry efforts in such a way to overcome or even mitigate this problem. This is the work of the Holy Spirit alone as he applies the proclamation of Christ.

THE FOCUS OF ORDINARY GOSPEL PROCLAMATION

It is precisely because we cannot overthrow satanic deception or the grip sin has on idolaters that the missionary remains doggedly focused on Christ-centered preaching. Ministers of Christ do not preach themselves to others. Pastors have nothing salvific in themselves to offer their congregations, nor do missionaries have anything salvific in themselves to offer the nations. Inasmuch as we believe we have something to offer, we begin to tamper with the Word of God. In blasphemous pride we search for ways to soften the blow of biblical truth—to repackage Christ and his church in a manner that sells what the world is buying. Paul told us what we are to preach: "For what we proclaim is not ourselves, but Jesus Christ as Lord, with ourselves as your servants for Jesus' sake. For God, who said, 'Let light shine out of darkness,' has shone in our hearts to give the light of the knowledge of the glory of God in the face of Jesus Christ" (2 Cor 4:5–6).

We are servants who proclaim Christ. We are ambassadors on behalf of Christ's kingdom who represent him to a lost and dying world as their only hope of reconciliation with God (2 Cor 5:18–21). Paul's language of proclaiming Christ is a summary statement for preaching the covenant grace of God that was first promised in Genesis 3:15 and progressively unfolded throughout the Scriptures until it reached its full and final revelation in the incarnation, life, death, resurrection, ascension, and return of our Lord Jesus Christ.[4] The missionary ought to be committed to preaching Christ to the exclusion of all else (1 Cor 2:2). Commenting on this text, William Carey and his ministry companions wrote, "It would be very easy for a missionary to preach nothing but truths, and that for many years together, without any well-grounded hope of becoming useful to one soul. The doctrine of Christ's expiatory death and all-sufficient merits has been, and must ever remain, the grand mean of conversion. This doctrine, and others immediately connected with it, have constantly nourished and sanctified the church."[5]

We preach Christ because we believe that the same God who spoke the universe into existence will make others a new creation in Christ (2 Cor 5:17). He who told the light to be, and it was, is he who shines the light of the knowledge of the glory of God in the face of Jesus Christ into our hearts (2 Cor 4:6). The Father is revealed to us in the Son incarnate (John 1:14, 18). The Father makes the Son known to us by the Holy Spirit through the ordinary means of gospel proclamation (Matt 11:25–27; Rom 10:14–17; 1 Cor 2:1–14). God uses this ordinary means to bring about extraordinarily gracious salvation in Christ.

---

4 This is precisely why we commend chronological Bible storytelling—unfolding the gospel story by moving from creation in Genesis to new creation in Christ—for unreached peoples. The groundwork for God, man, sin, and Christ must be laid (Luke 24:44–46; Heb 1:1–2). See ch. 6; see 2LCF 7 and WCF 7.
5 *Serampore Form of Agreement*, article 5.

APPLICATION

The paradoxical nature of gospel ministry is found in the fact that ordinary vessels contain an extraordinary treasure. Men who are weak carry a powerful message: "But we have this treasure in jars of clay, to show that the surpassing power belongs to God and not to us" (2 Cor 4:7). The incongruity between our nature as jars of clay and the gospel as God's treasure could not be greater. No one puts their treasure into a common and weak vessel. Vessels that are breakable are not worthy of holding the immeasurably powerful treasure of the gospel of Jesus Christ. Why does God then place this great treasure into weak jars of clay? He does precisely for the purpose of demonstrating that the power of gospel ministry is not found in the gospel minister but in the God of the gospel (Col 1:28–29).

Ordinary gospel preaching is uniquely powerful in a way that merely human methodologies are not. Like Bob Brady—or the authors themselves early in our ministries—the sincerest believers in Christ will be faced with the temptation to replace the simplicity of gospel proclamation with new methods that promise to soften the gospel's offense. But none of these methods is attended to with the unique promise of the Spirit's blessing and superintendence. We must resist this temptation. If we could find alternative evangelistic methods that actually worked, people's faith would no longer rest exclusively on God (1 Cor 2:5). John Gill cuts to the heart of this:

> The reason why it pleased God to put such a rich and valuable treasure into the hands of persons so mean and contemptible was, that the excellency of the power may be of God, and not of us; that is, that it might appear that the making of such persons ministers of the word was not of themselves, was not owing to their natural abilities, or to any diligence and industry, and acquirements of their own, or to any instructions they had received from others, but to the grace of God, and the effectual working of his power; and that the success which attended their ministrations in the conversion of sinners, and building up of saints, could only be ascribed to the exceeding greatness of divine power; and that the supporting of them

in their work, under all the persecutions raised against them, and opposition made unto them, could be attributed to nothing else.⁶

STUDY QUESTIONS

1. What is the ordinary means of gospel ministry to which a missionary must be committed?

2. What methods of gospel ministry must a missionary repudiate with extreme bias? What are some forms these methods might take today?

3. In 1923, J. Gresham Machen wrote,

   > According to modern liberalism, faith is essentially the same as 'making Christ Master' in one's life; at least it is by making Christ Master in the life that the welfare of men is sought. But that simply means that salvation is thought to be obtained by our own obedience to the commands of Christ. Such teaching is just a sublimated form of legalism. Not the sacrifice of Christ, on this view, but our own obedience to God's law, is the ground of hope. In this way the whole achievement of the Reformation has been given up, and there has been a return to the religion of the Middle Ages.⁷

4. How does the "obedience-based discipleship" model inherent in disciple-making movements provide a new version of early twentieth-century liberalism?

5. In your view, are insider movements, with their emphasis on keeping new Christian converts in their original religious contexts so as not to disrupt their families and societies, "tampering with God's word" and thus practicing "disgraceful and underhanded" ways (to borrow Paul's language)? Why or why not?

---

6 Gill, *An Exposition of the New Testament*, 780.
7 Machen, *Christianity and Liberalism*, 143.

6. Is the goal of the missionary task to improve people or to make people new? What does it mean to make them new? Who does this converting and transforming work (1 Cor 2:1–14; 2 Cor 3:5)?[8]

---

8 See 2LCF 20.4.

9

THE GLORIOUS REWARD
IN MISSIONS

*For this light momentary affliction is preparing for us an
eternal weight of glory beyond all comparison.*
2 Corinthians 4:17

When missionaries Todd and Jennifer DeKryger celebrated the opening of their new mission hospital in West Africa, they never dreamed that a year later Todd would be medevacked to Germany and admitted to a hospital for the first time in his life.

Todd, a surgeon and chief of staff at Hospital of Hope in Mango, Togo, was known to all his teammates and supporters for his charisma, spiritual leadership, and passion for the unreached Muslim peoples of northern Togo. So, when the DeKrygers announced that Todd had contracted an unusual infection and was not responding to treatment, prayers and support flooded in. Yet Todd's condition worsened. Barely conscious, Todd bade farewell to his sons while being loaded on a plane to Cologne, Germany. Less than two weeks after first contracting Lassa fever, the forty-six-year-old missionary slipped into eternity.[1]

Left to raise four children in a third-world country, Jennifer was left with a choice: stay and minister or return home. We will consider her decision later. But for now, her example is sufficient to illustrate

---

1 The full account is recorded in Naomi Harward, "Don't Waste Your Grief," *Message Magazine* (volume 68, issue 2), July 2018, 10–21.

that *the missionary call is a call to suffer*. From the ordinary struggles of life overseas to the extreme trials of loss or imprisonment, to take the gospel to the nations is to enlist for hardship.

Jesus warns that anyone who would follow him should be prepared to forsake all worldly attachments (Luke 14:26–33). When he first sent out his disciples on mission in Israel, he punctuated his sober instructions: "Whoever does not take his cross and follow me is not worthy of me" (Matt 10:38). The example of the apostles illustrates that faithfulness often precedes persecution, suffering, and even martyrdom. Perhaps the life of the apostle Paul provides the most vivid illustration. Paul tells the Corinthians that he was "afflicted in every way, . . . perplexed, . . . persecuted, . . . struck down, . . . always carrying in the body the death of Jesus" (2 Cor 4:8–10). Gospel ministers must be prepared for affliction.

When was the last time you saw a missions organization speak candidly in this way? Have you ever seen a sending agency advertise the opportunity to carry "the death of Jesus" in your own body? What short-term missions trip offers a chance to be "afflicted in every way"? This is no light matter. Much of modern missionary mobilization has become virtually indiscernible from tourist marketing. Prospective missionaries are promised that by traveling abroad they can realize their full personal potential. Workers then arrive on the field with an inflated view of self and an unhealthy craving for self-actualization—expectations shattered by the pain and toil of language learning, team conflict, homesickness, physical illness, culture shock, and spiritual warfare. They return home dejected, sometimes having done harm to the cause of Christ on the field—or, worse yet, they stay on the field and remain unfruitful. The church at home needs a wake-up call if we are to faithfully engage our missionary task.

What enables endurance through such turmoil?

AN ETERNAL WEIGHT OF GLORY

It is easy for our perception of Paul to take on a storybook quality. We envision a larger-than-life apostle gallivanting around the Roman world witnessing nonstop success. But Paul was refreshingly candid about his missionary suffering. We see Paul's honesty about both his pain and his source of comfort in 2 Corinthians 4:16–18: "So we do not lose heart. Though our outer self is wasting away, our inner self is being renewed day by day. For this light momentary affliction is preparing for us an eternal weight of glory beyond all comparison, as we look not to the things that are seen but to the things that are unseen. For the things that are seen are transient, but the things that are unseen are eternal."

Paul is not dismissive of his hardships, and he is under no illusion that mere positive thinking could somehow change his outward circumstances. Paul would have been no friend to the modern prosperity heresy that teaches God always wants us to be healthy and wealthy, nor to the softer self-help version that predominates evangelicalism. His sufferings were not insignificant. But Paul's sufferings *were* insignificant compared with the "eternal weight of glory" awaiting him.

Citing 1 Corinthians 4:9–13 and 2 Corinthians 11:23–29, the nineteenth-century Princetonian theologian Charles Hodge insightfully remarked the following:

> Viewed absolutely, or in comparison with the sufferings of other men, Paul's afflictions were exceedingly great. He was poor, often without food or clothing; his body was weak and sickly; he was homeless; he was beset by cruel enemies; he was repeatedly scourged, he was stoned, he was imprisoned, he was shipwrecked, robbed, and counted as the off scouring of the earth; he was beyond measure harassed by anxieties and cares, and by the opposition of false teachers, and the corruption of the churches which he had planted at such expense of time and labour. . . . These afflictions in themselves, and as they affected Paul's consciousness, were exceedingly great; for he says himself he was pressed out of measure, above strength, so that he despaired even of life. . . . He did not regard these afflictions as trifles, nor did he bear them with stoical indifference. He felt their full force and pressure. When five times scourged by the Jews and thrice beaten with rods, his physical torture was as keen as that which any other man would have

suffered under similar inflictions. He was not insensible to hunger, and thirst, and cold, and contempt, and ingratitude. His afflictions were not light in the sense of giving little pain. . . . It was only by bringing these sufferings into comparison with eternal glory that they dwindled into insignificance. So also when the apostle says that his afflictions were for a moment, it is only when compared with eternity. They were not momentary so far as the present life was concerned. They lasted from his conversion to his martyrdom. His Christian life was a protracted dying. But what is the longest life to everlasting ages? . . . We are, therefore, not to seek afflictions, but when God sends them we should rejoice in them as the divinely appointed means of securing for us an eternal weight of glory.[2]

For Paul, the prize was worth the fight. Elsewhere he writes, "For I consider that the sufferings of this present time are not worth comparing with the glory that is to be revealed to us" (Rom 8:18). We encounter this same theology of suffering throughout the New Testament. Jesus himself endured the cross "for the joy that was set before him" (Heb 12:2). For saints and martyrs through the ages, only in view of "the things that are unseen"—things eternally weighty and glorious—can one endure the adversities of faithful, missional service to God.

What are these unseen things? We may consider three such realities.

Refinement of Our Character

In Psalm 119, in which King David praises God's law at length, he also commends his own affliction. In verse 67, he sings, "Before I was afflicted I went astray, but now I keep your word." He repeats in verse 71, "It is good for me that I was afflicted, that I might learn your statutes." David's suffering was good, not because he was a masochist but because it resulted in his own personal sanctification. The flames of trial purged away his worldly desires and refined his affections for God's law, causing him to persevere in holiness. This is what Paul means in Romans 5: "We rejoice in our sufferings, knowing that suffering

---

2 Charles Hodge, *An Exposition of the Second Epistle to the Corinthians* (New York: A. C. Armstrong & Son, 1891), 103–104.

produces endurance, and endurance produces character, and character produces hope" (vv. 3–4).

Sufferings can only refine the character of the missionary if he realizes they are not random but that an omnipotent, sovereign Lord foreordained them as a tool for his ultimate good. Sufferings are not merely "used" by God to sanctify us as though God had to play the hand dealt to him by some cosmic card dealer. Rather, God *intends* whatever happens to us. Sufferings sanctify us because they are filtered through the sovereign hands of our all-good, all-wise God. William Carey spent more than twenty years translating Scripture into a variety of Indian languages, yet his life's work was lost in mere hours when a fire engulfed his print shop in 1812. In a letter reporting the tragedy to Andrew Fuller, his key sending pastor, he reflected on Psalm 46:10 ("Be still, and know that I am God. I will be exalted among the nations, I will be exalted in the earth!") and concluded this: "1. God has a sovereign right to dispose of us as he pleases. 2. We ought to acquiesce in all that God does with us and to us."[3] This attitude only comes from a missionary convinced that sufferings are expressly ordained by a loving Father whose purpose it is to conform us to the image of Christ (Rom 8:28–29).

Even here, however, is an error we must avoid: that of embracing missionary life simply to achieve some mythical level of personal spirituality. We see this in the number of missionary candidates who describe their sense of calling in exclusively individualistic terms—"I feel like I need to do this for my life to matter," or "I have this constant yearning to travel overseas," or "I won't be satisfied unless I do something more meaningful than my current occupation." The problem with these responses is that they all share one subject: the self. Such thinking, untampered by consideration of God's glory or the plight of the lost, demonstrates a lack of perspective. It is commendable to find one's satisfaction in service to God, but there are easier ways to do this

---

3 Eustace Carey, *Memoir of William Carey, D. D.: Late Missionary to Bengal; Professor of Oriental Languages in the College of Fort William, Calcutta* (Boston: Gould, Kendall and Lincoln, 1836), 525.

that do not put the souls of others on the line. The character-building sufferings of missions must not be undertaken merely as an exercise in some self-serving spiritual fitness regimen.

The trials and difficulties of missions indeed serve to sanctify the missionary, but this is not the only glorious, unseen reality to pursue.

Redemption of Our Hearers

We suffer not for mere personal benefit but for others. God is the ultimate cause of the salvation of his people, but he utilizes instrumental means in that process. In the economy of God, the suffering of gospel workers is one such means used to accomplish the salvation of the church. Missionaries suffer so that Christ's people may be assembled into the community of the redeemed.

As we return to 2 Corinthians 4, recall that Paul said that his suffering for the gospel was "all for your sake, so that as grace extends to more and more people it may increase thanksgiving, to the glory of God" (2 Cor 4:15). This glorious multiplying of worship refers to the upbuilding and spreading of the church as the people of God. Paul also wrote to Timothy, "I endure everything for the sake of the elect, that they also may obtain the salvation that is in Christ Jesus with eternal glory" (2 Tim 2:10). In Colossians, Paul is even more explicit: "I rejoice in my sufferings for your sake, and in my flesh I am filling up what is lacking in Christ's afflictions for the sake of his body, that is, the church" (Col 1:24). Paul's pain didn't add to the finished work of Christ, but it commended his message to his hearers. Paul conducted his ministry "in weakness and in fear and much trembling . . . in demonstration of the Spirit and of power" so that the faith of his hearers "might not rest in the wisdom of men but in the power of God" (1 Cor 2:3–5). His pain was the black velvet that cast his shining gospel into stark relief.

Several years ago, Wayne and Gail Chen were missionaries serving among the Biem people group in Papua New Guinea, having prepared for years to reach the unevangelized tribe with the gospel. Months before their team was to present the gospel to the Biem for the first time in history, the Chens learned that Gail had cancer. The necessary surgery, chemotherapy, and radiation required Gail to be in Taiwan. Gail urged Wayne to return to the Biem without her, if necessary, and he did—on multiple occasions. All this prompted a member of the Biem tribe to remark, "I have no idea what you guys are going to tell me, but it must be pretty important, because you guys are still coming back even with the illness." At the time of this writing, Gail's cancer has reached stage 4, having metastasized throughout her body. Yet how can we but marvel at the door opened among the Biem on account of the Chens' trials? When the lost and unreached see the servants of God suffer gladly to bring them the gospel, the Spirit of God is often pleased to open hearts and minds to grasp the surpassing worth of Christ.

Resurrection of Our Bodies

Faithful missionaries do not endure suffering for temporal benefits. They endure in view of what Paul describes next:

> For we know that if the tent that is our earthly home is destroyed, we have a building from God, a house not made with hands, eternal in the heavens. For in this tent we groan, longing to put on our heavenly dwelling, if indeed by putting it on we may not be found naked. For while we are still in this tent, we groan, being burdened—not that we would be unclothed, but that we would be further clothed, so that what is mortal may be swallowed up by life. He who has prepared us for this very thing is God, who has given us the Spirit as a guarantee. (2 Cor 5:1–5)

We should not let Paul's understated language mislead us; these are issues of life and death. His "tent" and "clothes" refer to his physical body. By "destroying" the tent or "putting off" his clothing, he refers to his own death, at which point he would be with the Lord in heaven (v. 6). And by "putting on" his heavenly dwelling, or "further clothing" himself, he refers to the glorious final day of human history on which believers will be raised from the dead to live with Christ forever (4:14).

Paul is not being melodramatic. In Asia Minor he had despaired of life itself and felt that death was imminent (1:8–9). In the last chapter, we considered Paul's other statements in this epistle to the effect that he was a jar of clay, vexed on all sides by weakness and pain (4:7–12). Church history tells us that Paul would be beheaded under Emperor Nero about a decade after penning 2 Corinthians. The threat of death was real. So, for Paul, only the exceeding glory of the final day of resurrection could ultimately outweigh his present affliction.

Our goal throughout this book has been to illustrate why theology matters to missions. We now arrive at one of the most controversial yet critical areas of biblical teaching: eschatology, the study of last things. Under this head of doctrine fall such teachings as the return of Christ, the circumstances surrounding the end of human history, and the nature of the eternal state. Every believer is called to live in light of the blessed hope: the appearance of Christ and the consummate realization of the promise of eternal life.

But far too often, when we consider eschatology, we are caught up in controversy over the identity of the antichrist, the mark of the beast in Revelation 13, or the meaning of the millennium in chapter 20. These issues, while important, often fail to keep in view the focus of all New Testament prophecy: the glorious achievement of Christ in consummating the work of redemption and renewing the cosmos. In our short-sightedness, we forget that the book of Revelation is just as much—if not more—of a handbook of suffering and endurance as it is a guide for future events:

- The apostle John writes from exile on the isle of Patmos and introduces himself as a "partner in the tribulation and the kingdom and the patient endurance that are in Jesus" (Rev 1:9).
- The book begins with letters to seven key churches throughout Asia Minor, several of which are about to undergo intense tribulation. Jesus specifically tells the church in Smyrna not to fear the persecution they are

about to suffer (2:10). Each church address closes with a promise of blessing to those who "conquer."

- God's elect from all nations are identified as those delivered through great tribulation (7:9, 14).
- In 12:11, we learn that the saints of God "have conquered him [Satan] by the blood of the Lamb and by the word of their testimony, for they loved not their lives even unto death."
- In the final movement of the book, we receive a glimpse into a consummated new creation in which God "will wipe away every tear from their eyes, and death shall be no more, neither shall there be mourning, nor crying, nor pain anymore, for the former things have passed away" (21:4).

The whole body of biblical teaching regarding eschatology is a gift given to the church to enable faithful, death-defying missionary obedience. But our understanding of last things will not function in this way if we are tossed about on the waves of sensationalism, controversy, or contemporary geopolitical concerns foreign to the thinking of Scripture's authors. We must be equipped with a biblical understanding of the goal of history and the hope awaiting believers.

THE ALL-IMPORTANT CONSUMMATION

Throughout the history of the church, few councils or creeds have gone much further in addressing the return of Christ than the formulation found in the Apostles' Creed—that Christ "shall come to judge the living and the dead" and bring about the "resurrection of the body."[4] Other confessional documents like the Westminster Confession of Faith expand on this: "At the last day, such as are found alive shall not die, but be changed: and all the dead shall be raised up, with the selfsame bodies, and none other (although with different qualities), which shall be united again to their souls for ever. . . . The bodies of the unjust

---
4 The Apostles' Creed, version c. AD 542.

shall, by the power of Christ, be raised to dishonour: the bodies of the just, by His Spirit, unto honour; and be made conformable to His own glorious body."[5]

These simple truths are nonnegotiable. Beyond these assertions, however, there is wisdom in holding our convictions concerning future events with an open hand. We must begin from a standpoint of creaturely humility. God is God, and we are not. The secret things belong to God; only the revealed things are ours to obey (Deut 29:29). Scripture presents few details concerning the eternal state. If even the Son of Man in his earthly humiliation chose to lay aside his access to knowledge of some future events (Matt 24:36), how much more limited are we?

Yet we cannot mistake humble open-mindedness about Christ's return with total agnosticism. Scripture has clear teachings for us. Eschatology matters. Christ's return is not an appendage to the gospel but its crowning pinnacle. If Christ were not to return, then we would have redemption without restoration, kingdom without consummation, justification without vindication, and seed without harvest.

When I (Alex) interview missionary candidates on doctrine, I often address eschatology with this question first: Why is it necessary that Christ return *bodily*? The answer has at least in part to do with our Lord's ascension in Acts 1, where these angelic words are recorded for us: "This Jesus, who was taken up from you into heaven, will come in the same way as you saw him go into heaven" (v. 11). Note the phrase "in the same way." Because Jesus ascended to rule the universe in a glorified body and has promised to return in that *same* glorified body to receive his consummated kingdom, then we have certainty that his appearing will be visible, physical, and cataclysmic—not merely symbolic, spiritual, or secret. If the return of Christ is not literal and bodily, God is a liar. Whoever denies the physical return of Christ on the last day is guilty of grave heresy and will be caught tragically off-guard on that day.

---

5 WFC (1647) 32.2–3.

What should we expect at the return of Christ? For the unbelieving, the appearance of Christ will be the terrifying opening sequence to an eternity of torment. In 2 Thessalonians we read of "the righteous judgment of God . . . when the Lord Jesus is revealed from heaven with his mighty angels in flaming fire, inflicting vengeance on those who do not know God and on those who do not obey the gospel of our Lord Jesus . . . [and] the punishment of eternal destruction, away from the presence of the Lord and from the glory of his might" (1:5, 7–9). Yet those in Christ are promised nothing less than that we will be raised from the dead in sinless bodies conformed to the glory of the risen Christ himself (Acts 24:15; John 5:28, 29; Rom 8:21; 1 Cor 15:21–23; Phil 3:21). Whereas the unbelieving dead will be raised to eternal torment, believers will receive bodies fitted to experience the personal presence of God: "Beloved, we are God's children now, and what we will be has not yet appeared; but we know that when he appears we shall be like him, because we shall see him as he is" (1 John 3:2).

And just as Christ died and rose, so also the whole created order will undergo its own death and rebirth under his reign. The whole cosmos will be renewed, conquered by Jesus, and made suitable for habitation by his resurrected saints. Jesus came to save the world (John 3:17), so we should not expect anything less than the full and final reconciliation of *this* created order to himself.

WHY MISSIONS IS ESCHATOLOGICAL

Even nonbelievers recognize the reality that those who labor and lead effectively do so with an eye toward ultimate ends. Business leadership expert Stephen Covey notes that highly effective people "begin with the end in mind," which means "to begin each day, task, or project with a clear vision of your desired direction and destination, and then continue by flexing your proactive muscles to make things happen."[6] In the same way, missionaries live in light of the day when the Great Commission will have been completed, the knowledge of the Lord will

---

6 "Habit 2: Begin With the End in Mind," FranklinCovey, accessed October 10, 2020, https://www.franklincovey.com/the-7-habits/habit-2.html.

saturate the earth (Hab 2:14), and Christ will deliver his kingdom to the Father. (1 Cor 15:24).

The missionary task is eschatological because it can only be accomplished with an eye toward eternity. We do not know the day or hour of our Lord's coming, and there is much of the mission left to be fulfilled first. But our lives are vapor, and our coming *to him* could happen at any moment. We will all soon face the Lord. Because Christ will raise and reward all who have suffered and labored for his name, we can "be steadfast, immovable, always abounding in the work of the Lord, knowing that in the Lord [our] labor is not in vain" (1 Cor 15:58).

APPLICATION

Three important aspects of the believer's resurrection bear immediate application to the missionary enterprise. First, the glory that awaits us is *physical*. The ancient Gnostic heretics insisted that the body and the physical world were inherently evil, and many evangelicals today fall into this same trap of thinking. But we are not Gnostics. We will not live in heaven forever as disembodied spirits. God called the physical world "good" (Gen 1:31), and he intends for us to exist forever as embodied souls, just as Christ our Lord remains forever in his corporeal existence.

Because the glory that awaits us is tangible, we know that the material realm matters to God. The deeds done in the body matter. While this world is temporary, what we do with it has eternal reverberations. Hence, while missions should always prioritize evangelism, it does not exclude acts of mercy and compassion aimed to improve the physical welfare of others. Paul, when called to preach the gospel, was "eager" to remember the poor (Gal 2:10). True religion consists partly in care for the orphan and widow (Jas 1:27). Missionaries must care for the physical needs of the lost. Missions is not synonymous with humanitarian relief, but it is no coincidence that the areas of the greatest global poverty overlap considerably with the places of least gospel access. Where the news of Christ's death, resurrection, reign, and return is believed and obeyed, the earthly lot of man is improved through culture-shaping acts of love.

Second, the glory that awaits us is *future*. This should go without saying, but it bears repeating because far too often we fall prey to the false expectation of satisfaction in this present life. This is particularly true within large elements of the Pentecostal and charismatic movements, whose adherents ballooned worldwide from less than 1 million in 1900 to some 500 million by 2000.[7] While much of this growth represents sincere followers of Christ, it has occurred in tandem with a surge of dangerous false teachers with a similar emphasis on the supernatural to obtain worldly blessing. The prosperity "gospel" and "word of faith" movement promises that God always wills for his people to be healthy, wealthy, and happy and that the only thing preventing such blessings is insufficient faith. This heresy overlaps considerably with many of the world's tribal religious traditions. Any missionary today serving in Africa, Asia, or Latin America is likely to encounter these movements directly. Pernicious prosperity teachings threaten the souls of millions by replacing the glory of Christ with a pursuit of earthly treasure. Christ's atonement did secure physical healing for us in the sense that it secured our future resurrection from the dead, but it did not purchase any sort of unconditional promise of physical health in this life. When we preach the gospel, we must be careful to instruct our hearers that the reward secured by Christ is future and eternal, not immediate and temporal.

We often imbibe the unstated assumption that our faithfulness will always result in earthly comfort. Evangelical subculture makes much of having "abundant life" but precious little of the cruciform life. It is no wonder that we proliferate exotic, short-term missions trips while the number of long-term, risk-taking, pioneer missionaries remains few. Rather than speaking candidly as Paul did about suffering, we make it our aim to "thrive."[8] We have become too soft. It was only in

---

7   Costi W. Hinn and Anthony G. Wood, *Defining Deception: Freeing the Church from the Mystical-Miracle Movement* (El Cajon: Southern California Seminary Press, 2018), 11.

8   This is a theme to which the next chapter will return.

view of the eternal weight of glory that Ignatius of Antioch was able to pen such words as these in the second century as he was on his way to martyrdom in Rome: "Now I begin to be a disciple.... Let fire and the cross; let the crowds of wild beasts; let tearings, breakings, and dislocations of bones; let cutting off of members; let shatterings of the whole body; and let all the dreadful torments of the devil come upon me: only let me attain to Jesus Christ."[9] Nothing is more toxic to missionary endurance than a false expectation of temporal ease and security. By remembering that the promised glory is yet future, we guard our souls against the love of security that suffocates mission.

Finally, the glory that awaits us is *infinite*. The eternal state does not end. This is a simple concept. Yet how often do we allow it to truly impress itself on our imagination? Take a moment to do that right now as you read. Ponder for a moment the prospect of life with God that is literally *everlasting*. Human language fails us, as it did Paul: "What no eye has seen, nor ear heard, nor the heart of man imagined, what God has prepared for those who love him" (1 Cor 2:9; see also Isa 64:4). We cannot contemplate these realities too often.

Heaven and hell are real, and they are forever. A faithful missionary is one who gives time to consider such things. It is worth again citing the words of William Carey and his compatriots in their *Forms of Agreement*: "Oh that these glorious truths may ever be the joy and strength of our own souls, and then they will not fail to become the matter of our conversation to others."[10]

Our sober endurance depends on contemplating the fate of souls. When we do so, we place a needed check on our human impatience. We are often too hasty to send warm bodies to the field, regardless of their qualifications. Then, when difficulty or risk arises, we are quick to bring our sent ones home. We would do better to recognize missions

---

9 Ignatius, "The Epistle of Ignatius to the Romans," trans. Alexander Roberts and James Donaldson, from *Ante-Nicene Fathers*, vol. 1, ed. Alexander Roberts, James Donaldson, and A. Cleveland Coxe (Buffalo, NY: Christian Literature, 1885.). Rev. and ed. for New Advent by Kevin Knight, http://www.newadvent.org/fathers/0107.htm.

10 *Serampore Form of Agreement*, article 5.

as a marathon and not a sprint. But if we keep the fate of souls in view, we can gladly dedicate extra time to training or enduring a few more hard years of labor before returning home.

Jennifer DeKryger, left in Togo with her sons, had this eternal perspective. After an outpouring of compassion and support from friends, family, and her sending church following Todd's death, Jennifer and her family completed their furlough and returned to the field. In a 2018 interview, she described how she was enabled to endure:

> Before Todd went to glory, . . . our family was really thriving. . . . But I can strongly say that I've never desperately needed the presence of Christ in my life like I need it now. . . . [Now] I've found the greatest joy, the greatest comfort, in being able to speak those [gospel] truths from the word into the lives of my [Muslim] friends. That has been therapy for our souls. Why would we want to remove ourselves from a situation where we're finding the greatest joy, the greatest hope, and the greatest opportunities to speak truth?[11]

"Why leave the field now?" Jennifer says in effect. Through suffering, Jennifer experienced greater personal sanctification, more evangelistic opportunities, and closer conformity to her Lord. This is nothing less than what we found to be true with Paul in 2 Corinthians. And this surpassing weight of glory remains the prize for all faithful missionaries today who endure in light of the end.

STUDY QUESTIONS

1. What are some ways Christians tend to glamorize missionary life? How does Scripture depict a life devoted to gospel proclamation?

---

11 Scott Dunford and Alex Kocman, "Serving Christ in Suffering: Jenn DeKryger on Togo and the Loss of Todd DeKryger," August 27, 2018, in *The Missions Podcast*, podcast, https://missionspodcast.com/podcast/serving-christ-in-suffering-jenn-dekryger-on-togo-and-the-loss-of-todd-dekryger.

2. Paul spoke of his missionary sufferings as preparing for him an unseen glory of eternal weight and importance. What are some of these glorious, unseen things?
3. How does suffering sanctify the missionary? How can the missionary's suffering affect those he is serving?
4. What specific biblical points of doctrine concerning eschatology are nonnegotiable from a biblical standpoint? Why?
5. What does eschatology have to do with suffering?
6. What is the blessed hope of the believer? How does this impact the priority the missionary gives to temporal concerns like poverty and prosperity?

10

THE MISSIONARY COMMISSIONED TO ALL THE NATIONS

Think over what I say, for the Lord will give you understanding in everything.
2 Timothy 2:7

"I want my family to thrive in ministry. So, I bought my wife a really nice diamond ring."

I will never forget that line reverberating in my ears as I (Chad) sat in a conference on urban church planting. A young church planter was advising other pastors on the need to help their wives and children thrive in ministry in difficult places. He told us how his children needed to be educated in contexts outside the area where he was ministering, how his wife needed extravagant gifts and lush vacations, and how he was going to "transform the city." This was all in service to the objective of "thriving" in ministry.

To *thrive* is to flourish. We rightly desire that our children thrive physically, morally, and spiritually. We correctly desire to see marriages and churches thrive. We pray for the members of Christ's church to receive grace upon grace in Christ Jesus so their faith grows and thrives. Without a bit of hesitation, I affirm that I intensely desire that the young missionaries we send to the nations thrive. But a subtle turn in the use of that word concerns me. This turn is toward a kind of prosperity gospel, as was mentioned in the previous chapter.

Thriving increasingly takes on the freight of living an extraordinary, world-changing life.

An ordinary life is apparently insufficient for the Christian. It has become commonplace among modern evangelicals to eschew the sufficiency of faithfully surviving in lieu of living our best life now. This is because believers have embraced an erroneous understanding of what it means to flourish. Biblically, to "thrive" is to "faithfully endure" in our gospel calling in the face of much suffering, as we look to our heavenly reward (Heb 10:32–39). Blessed is the man who continues looking to Christ and rejoicing in suffering for his name (Matt 5:2–12). There are no commands for gospel ministers to transform cities or catalyze movements. Gospel ministers are called to the ordinary life of godliness and gospel proclamation (1 Tim 4:6–16).

This turn toward a prosperity gospel has a troubling effect in the way we see the missionaries we send to the nations. We begin to expect them to do far better than enduring in ordinary godliness and gospel ministry. They must be extraordinary world-changers. It is not enough for them to walk in godliness, proclaim Christ truthfully, and plant a church. This is a tragic misunderstanding of the nature of what the missionary is commissioned by the church to do.

We are commissioning missionaries to a deeply serious task. Thus, we bear much responsibility in qualifying, training, and supporting those we send. Three considerations must remain foremost in our minds as we contemplate commissioning missionaries. First, the missionary and his family will suffer great personal loss.[1] Second, the peoples to whom we send missionaries are condemned in their sin and need to hear the gospel clearly articulated if they will be saved. Third, we must be committed to sending missionaries whose lives and doctrine will bring honor to the Lord and his Word. We are sending people to the ends of the earth to put their hand to the plow of the most difficult

---

[1] While this chapter will often use the masculine singular third-person pronoun, this is not an indictment against, nor intention to exclude, women as missionaries. The primary reason for this choice is to harmonize my description of a missionary with Paul's instruction to Timothy.

calling a Christian disciple can engage. We want to send missionaries who will faithfully endure in godly living and sound doctrine. We do not want our missionaries to reflect a lie in their manner of living nor speak falsely about our Lord and Savior, Jesus Christ.

The apostle Paul understood the need to send the best and brightest young gospel ministers. He did not send out church members he could afford to lose. He sent out young men who were a great blessing to his personal ministry (1 Tim 1:2–3; 2 Tim 1:2–5). Paul sent men like Timothy—men who were godly (1 Tim 4:12), gifted (4:13–14), and well-trained in the doctrines of the faith (4:6, 16). After Paul sent Timothy, he wrote him two letters. In the second letter, Paul encouraged him to prepare for long-term, faithful endurance in gospel ministry in four ways—ways that we should apply to the missionaries our churches send today.

THE MISSIONARY MUST BE PREPARED TO PERSEVERE IN GOSPEL GRACE

Paul begins 2 Timothy 2:1 with an emphatic and deeply personal statement: "You then, my child, be strengthened by the grace that is in Christ Jesus." Paul had just written about men who failed to endure. Phygelus and Hermogenes did not persevere in gospel grace (2 Tim 1:15). As a father in the faith to Timothy and as a partner in the gospel ministry, Paul loved Timothy and did not want a similar outcome for him. Churches ought to hold this same deep concern for the young people we send to the nations. We should long for the missionaries we send out to persevere in gospel grace.

Paul's command to Timothy is to "be strengthened by the grace that is in Christ Jesus." The Greek verb "be strengthened" is an imperative that has a continuous and passive sense. The command is to be continually dependent on the Lord Jesus for strength. Timothy is being commanded to persevere in gospel ministry by reliance on the Father for the grace he has given us in Christ—grace sufficient for salvation and service in ministry. Christ Jesus has saved us (2 Tim 1:8–10). Christ Jesus is the one who sanctifies us for good works

(Eph 2:10), particularly for the good work of gospel ministry (2 Tim 1:11–14). The Father lovingly decreed to send his Son to save us (Eph 1:3–6). The Son came and purchased super-abounding grace for us in his life, death, and resurrection (Eph 1:7–12). The Holy Spirit was sent by the Father and the Son to apply that grace to us through faith (Eph 1:13–14). The triune Lord now indwells us by the Spirit (John 14:23; see also 14:16–17).

The same triune Lord sets apart gospel ministers as *heralds of this good news* that is to be preached to the nations. This should stupefy us! Who are we that God would speak his glorious redemptive Word through our mouths? We are creatures. How does the Creator deign to entrust us with his gospel? Moreover, we are but sinful creatures; how can God's Holy Word be spoken from our unclean lips? Further still, we are spiritually impotent in ourselves—there is no plan, program, or gimmick we can concoct that possesses any inherent power to change the heart. So, what power do we have in ourselves to be effective in gospel ministry? How can we stand in the battle against the world, the flesh, and the devil on behalf of Christ's people?

This is why the Spirit commands us to "be strengthened by the grace that is in Christ Jesus." This is trusting the power of God (2 Tim 1:8), relying on the sanctifying and empowering work of the Holy Spirit (2 Tim 1:14), and leaning on the grace we find in Christ. This is knowing that in the midst of our suffering for the gospel, our sufficiency comes from God, who makes us ministers of the new covenant (2 Cor 3:4–6).

How are missionaries continually strengthened by the grace in Christ Jesus? They are strengthened in God's grace through diligent attention to the ordinary means of grace God has given. The missionary is to be disciplined in being regularly in the Word and prayer. He knows he must persevere in grace first as a Christian in order to persevere in grace as a gospel minister. The missionary is a sheep before he is a shepherd. Missionaries must know they were first the enemies of God who were reconciled in Christ before they were those sent as ambassadors of reconciliation (2 Cor 5:11–21). Thus, the missionary's first sacred duty is to rely on Christ and be strengthened by his Spirit to persevere in gospel grace.

THE MISSIONARY MUST BE PREPARED TO PASS ON SOUND DOCTRINE TO FAITHFUL MEN

Paul next commands Timothy, "What you have heard from me in the presence of many witnesses entrust to faithful men, who will be able to teach others also" (2 Tim 2:2). Paul is speaking to his public ministry. Timothy is to entrust to faithful men the doctrine Paul publicly taught. Paul is not commanding Timothy to pass on some secret spiritual insight he received. He is also not commanding Timothy to encourage unbelievers to interpret Scripture on their own. Timothy is to pass on the apostolic doctrine handed down to him: "Follow the pattern of the sound words that you have heard from me, in the faith and love that are in Christ Jesus. By the Holy Spirit who dwells within us, guard the good deposit entrusted to you" (2 Tim 1:13–14).

The "pattern of sound words" Timothy is to follow is the doctrinal content that forms the "good deposit" Paul entrusted to Timothy. This is the apostolic doctrine passed to the church (Acts 2:42; see also 1 Cor 15:1–3) as its foundation (Eph 2:20), which is inscripturated in the Bible (2 Tim 3:14–16; 2 Pet 1:19–21). We receive and interpret the Word of God (Ezra 7:10), giving the proper sense of it to Christ's people (Neh 8:8) so that we hear what the Lord is saying to his people (2 Tim 4:1–4). This is why Christ gave pastors and teachers to his church (Eph 4:11–16).

Timothy is to follow that apostolic doctrine, teach that doctrine, and guard that doctrine with a heart devoted to the Lord by the effectual assistance of the Holy Spirit. Timothy has received this sound doctrine from Paul, and now Timothy is to take this doctrine and entrust it to faithful men who will be able to teach others also. To entrust the doctrine is to ensure the doctrine is kept safe for further public declaration. Think of this! The Lord has entrusted these gospel doctrines to your gospel ministers and missionaries, and even to you as a member of the church (Gal 1:6–9). Of this tremendous privilege, John Calvin said, "This gospel radiates his Glory; it is the kingly scepter by which he governs his people, and yet he hands it over to us!"[2]

The missionary is to take this sound doctrine entrusted to them and entrust it to "faithful men who are able to teach others also." "Faithful men" is not a reference to believers in general but to particular trustworthy and dependable men. This is referring to the kind of man with whom you leave what you consider most precious—a man you trust. These are the men we call as elders (Titus 1:9). Paul does not say to entrust these things to "charismatic, talented, popular men" or to men "who are good communicators, entertaining speakers" or to men "who are able to draw crowds with rhetorical power, worldly methods, or winsome personalities." Nor does Paul tell Timothy to simply entrust these things to "unconverted 'persons of peace' who know the language and culture better than you."[3]

The faithful men are setting an example for the believers "in speech, in conduct, in love, in faith, in purity" (1 Tim 4:12). They are men who follow the pattern of sound words (2 Tim 1:13) and rightly handle the word of truth (2 Tim 2:15). They are men devoted to the public reading of Scripture, to teaching, and to exhortation (1 Tim 4:13). They are men who are willing and able to teach sound doctrine and refute those who contradict (Titus 1:9), faithful men who decide to know nothing but Jesus Christ and him crucified (1 Cor 2:1–5) and are unashamed of the gospel, which they believe is the power of God for salvation (Rom 1:16). They are men with hearts humbled by the grace of God,

---

2 John Calvin, *Sermons on Second Timothy* (Carlisle, PA: Banner of Truth, 2018), 111.

3 "Persons of peace" is a term, adapted from Luke 10:6–7, used in disciple-making movements to describe someone friendly toward the Christian missionary and willing to facilitate a Discovery Bible Study in their home. While Scripture furnishes examples in redemptive history of new converts who were central to the conversion of households and communities, we believe the blanket application of the "person of peace" principle is misguided, especially when broadened to include unconverted unbelievers. For more, see Alex Kocman, "What Should We Do with 'Persons of Peace'?" *ABWE Blog*, ABWE International, October 2, 2019, https://www.abwe.org/blog/what-should-we-do-%E2%80%98persons-peace%E2%80%99.

minds captured by the verities of our triune Lord, and spines steeled by reverent fear of the Lord. These are the men who want to pick up the sword of the Spirit—the Word of God—and storm the gates of hell to rescue the lost. These are men whose knees are calloused from prayer, whose eyes are filled with tears for the weak and straying, and whose feet never tire of carrying the Word of God to the pulpit or from house to house (Acts 20:17–21). They are men who are ready to suffer the loss of all things that Jesus might be proclaimed in all nations— men who tirelessly remain on the alert to battle the wolves for the protection of the sheep (Acts 20:28–31). Those are the men to whom we entrust sound doctrine that they might teach others also.

MISSIONARIES MUST BE PREPARED TO PARTICIPATE IN SUFFERING FOR THE GOSPEL

When someone follows in the footsteps of our Lord in gospel ministry, they will inevitably suffer as he did. Suffering is not just something that happens occasionally for the missionary. Rather, suffering is the chosen, joyful lot of the missionary. Paul counted it his joy to suffer for the sake of Christ's name (Col 1:24). He commanded Timothy to join him in suffering for the gospel: "Share in suffering as a good soldier of Christ Jesus" (2 Tim 2:3; see also 1:8, 12; 2:9). The suffering Paul is addressing is persecution and opposition from the world, the flesh, and the devil.

This kind of suffering for the gospel is part and parcel to gospel ministry. We will be opposed as all the forces of hell are allied against Christ and his ministers. We are to embrace this suffering as Paul did, and as our Lord and Savior did. Satan will wage war against our missionaries and those they are reaching. And one of his most effective tools is to cause the missionary to flee or fall, whether through personal impiety, through impatience with the difficulties of the Christian life and ministry, or through deceitful doctrines.

To prepare Timothy, Paul provided three metaphors that help us understand what it looks like to participate in suffering with him as a gospel minister: "Share in suffering as a good soldier of Christ Jesus. No soldier gets entangled in civilian pursuits, since his aim is to please the one who enlisted him. An athlete is not crowned unless he competes according to the rules. It is the hard-working farmer who ought to have the first share of the crops" (2 Tim 2:3–6).

Paul's first metaphor for the gospel minister is that of an *undistracted soldier*. The good soldier of Christ Jesus does not get entangled in civilian pursuits—the concerns of this present world. This is not a call to monasticism whereby the missionary withdraws from this world and its concerns. This is a call to stay alert and avoid the daily distractions that inhibit our service to the Lord. The missionary must not allow worldly comforts and desires to distract him. In other words, Paul is calling for wholehearted devotion to the gospel ministry. The missionary is a soldier on active duty. The battle is waging. He is to be undistracted in devotion to this battle, though suffering might make it easy to long for greener pastures. But the good soldier stays in the battle because his aim is to please the Lord who enlisted him.

Paul's second metaphor for the gospel minister is a *rule-keeping athlete*. The athlete is to compete according to the rules so that he is not disqualified from receiving the prize. What are the rules in gospel ministry? The rules are quite simple: live a godly life and teach sound doctrine (2 Tim 1:13–14; 1 Tim 4:16). The missionary is to walk in holiness while teaching sound doctrine and refuting those who contradict (Titus 1:9). Paul did not run aimlessly but ran as one pursuing the prize, as one who disciplined himself, so that after preaching to others he would not find himself disqualified (1 Cor 9:24–27). This is why Paul can say at the end of his life that he has finished the race and will now receive the crown of righteousness (2 Tim 4:7–8).

Paul's third metaphor for the gospel minister is the *hardworking farmer*. The farmer exhausts himself in season and out of season with tilling, planting, watering, and harvesting the field. Like the farmer, missionaries are to work hard. It is all too easy in the quiet of your personal study to become lazy in attending to the Word and prayer. It is all too easy for the missionary in a foreign context, away from real scrutiny and accountability, to become lazy and distracted. Withdrawal and laziness are particularly tempting when you have been beaten up by difficulties in the ministry. The missionary can easily put aside the tedious and frustrating hours of language learning, the rigors of adapting to cultural differences, and the burden of being in the Word and prayer while he escapes into the world of social media where his heart is able to travel home through the medium of modern technology.

But the missionary is to diligently labor in the Word (2 Tim 2:15). He must also know the people to whom he is ministering so that he does not box as one beating in the air. He must put in the countless and exhausting hours of language and culture learning if he ever hopes to communicate the Word of God with clarity. He is to toil and strive in gospel ministry. He is to work with all God's strength that he powerfully works in us to proclaim Christ (Col 1:28–29). He is to pray, warn, teach, admonish, and exhort with all humility in tearful urgency (Acts 20:28–31). He is to do this work in public and from house to house with complete patience and teaching (Acts 20:17–21; 2 Tim 4:1–5).

Missionaries Must Be Prepared to Ponder Their Gospel Duty

Paul's fourth command to Timothy may be the most peculiar to our modern ears. Paul commanded Timothy to "think over what I say, for the Lord will give you understanding in everything" (2 Tim 2:7). This is a command to ponder and meditate on what Paul has been saying. He does not want Timothy's mind to divert from the Spirit-inspired Word to the tyranny of the urgent around him. He wants Timothy to fix his mind on what he is saying. The missionary must be challenged to ponder the verities of the gospel, the nature of his calling, and the reality of the suffering he faces. He needs to count the cost of his task (Luke 14:25–33). The missionary may lose his wife, child, or even his own life for the sake of the gospel. He will certainly lose his comfort, worldly wealth, and personal acclaim. Yet he is to remain faithful to his charge to preach the gospel. In the face of such suffering for the gospel, the missionary must set his mind on Christ and all his heavenly blessings (Col 3:1–4). The missionary must give himself fully to this gospel mission, knowing that Jesus is worth every hour of struggling to learn language and culture, every moment of effort in the Word and prayer, every loss of personal comfort and blessing in this world, and every tempting assault from Satan. As William Carey wrote, "Let us give ourselves up unreservedly to this glorious cause. Let us never think that our time, our gifts, our strength, our families, or even the clothes we wear, are our own. Let us sanctify them all to God and his cause. Oh! that he may sanctify us for his work."[4]

APPLICATION

We are sending people to the ends of the earth to complete a humanly impossible mission. It is a mission that requires the supernatural work of the Holy Spirit working through the means of his Word to convert men and women to new life and faith in Christ Jesus. This is a mission in which Christ's servants will suffer with him to make his name known in every tribe, tongue, and nation. They run this glorious race, forsaking worldly prizes and pleasures, with their eyes fixed on their eternal reward. These young people are not being sent out to invent new methods and measures, to practice cunning, or to tamper with God's Word (2 Cor 4:1–2). They are not commanded to seek a "fresh wind" of miraculous power by means of a missions practice heretofore unknown to Christ's church. Rather, they are to keep a close watch on themselves and on the doctrine (1 Tim 4:16).

In a day in which many evangelicals are taught that "every Christian is a missionary," we must nevertheless strive for a high bar of missionary qualification. Students and young adults who aspire to serve on the mission field must pay close attention to every aspect of their lives and character—not only their knowledge of Scripture and theology but their family lives, finances, and even physical fitness.[5] Missionaries

---

[4] *Serampore Form of Agreement*, article 11.
[5] This point cannot be overstated. For more on these practical considerations, see Alex Kocman, "College Students: Learn How to 'Adult' Before You 'Missionary,'" *ABWE Blog*, ABWE International, published January 1, 2021, https://www.abwe.org/blog/learn-how-'adult'-you-'missionary'.

may be sent out by the elders of the church while still tender, young, and relatively inexperienced, but they are sent as examples of healthy doctrine and life, devoted to competent teaching of the Scriptures, persistently practicing and immersing themselves in these things (1 Tim 4:11–15). The faithful missionary is an ambassador of Christ and his church, wholly committed to the biblical truth that sound doctrine and godly practice always walk together.

STUDY QUESTIONS

1. You have likely heard the joke that in Sunday school, "Jesus is always the answer." But we know that Jesus is only the answer if you are asking the right question. It is entirely possible to proclaim Christ and be heard by another people group in a manner far different than you intend. William Carey helped shape the *Serampore Form of Agreement*, which addressed this issue:

   > It is very important that we should gain all the information we can of the snares and delusions in which these heathens are held. By this means we shall be able to converse with them in an intelligible manner. To know their modes of thinking, their habits, their propensities, their antipathies, the way in which they reason about God, sin, holiness, the way of salvation, and a future state, to be aware of the bewitching nature of their idolatrous worship, feasts, songs, etc., is of the highest consequence, if we would gain their attention to our discourse, and would avoid being barbarians to them. This knowledge may be easily obtained by conversing with sensible natives, by reading some parts of their works and by attentively observing their manners and customs.[6]

2. What do we learn here about the magnitude and nature of the missionary's task?

---

6 Article 2.

3. In light of 2 Timothy 2:2, when is the missionary's work completed?

4. Given that a missionary must not be distracted by civilian affairs, what is the responsibility of the sending church in looking after the support and care of its missionaries?

5. Given that a missionary must teach sound doctrine and walk in godliness, what does this imply about the character, maturity, training, and assessing of those we send?

6. Given that a missionary must "compete according to the rules" (2 Tim 2:5), what are the implications to the ministry methods he employs?

7. A missionary is to be hardworking. The Serampore Form of Agreement addressed this as well:

> It becomes us to watch all opportunities of doing good. A missionary would be highly culpable if he contented himself with preaching two or three times a week to those persons whom he might be able to get together into a place of worship. To carry on conversations with the natives almost every hour in the day, to go from village to village, from market to market, from one assembly to another; to talk to servants, laborers, etc., as often as opportunity offers, and to be instant in season and out of season—this is the life to which we are called in this country. We are apt to relax in these active exertions, especially in a warm climate; but we shall do well always to fix it in our minds, that life is short, that all around are perishing.[7]

What are some ways you can identify whether a candidate is undistractedly hardworking? How could you train them toward further diligence in their vocation?

---

7 Article 4. Some special wording and punctuation are mine for the purpose of smoother reading.

Conclusion

Throughout this volume, we have sought to draw our missiology from the whole matrix of biblical doctrine from which it naturally springs. The doctrine of Scripture provides us with both the content of our proclamation and the sole and infallible standard by which our methods are to be judged. The doctrine of God builds in us an appreciation of his overflowing love for the world and a commitment to seeing the world respond to him in worship. The doctrine of Christ begets an understanding of the uniqueness of the Son's person, redemptive work, and authority, which must necessarily be reflected in the missionary's proclamation. The doctrine of the Holy Spirit leads us away from pragmatic human means toward a dependence on the Spirit's work of regeneration and sanctification to enable hearers of the gospel to believe and mature. The doctrine of the church establishes that it is God's will that his people be formed in visible, local congregations led by qualified men committed to the Word, fellowship, worship, prayer, sacrament, and mission. Inductive study of the apostles' example in the book of Acts establishes authoritative proclamation of the gospel as the normative means of disciple-making for the church through the ages. A robust, biblical theology of God's purposes for the nations, unfolded through redemptive history, renders a clear view of the audience of such proclamation. The doctrine of last things establishes the motivation underlying missionary endurance through suffering. And the wisdom imparted to young Timothy by the apostle Paul in his Pastoral Epistles shows the character essential to a missionary committed to sound doctrine and practice.

This survey has not been exhaustive in addressing each of the classical loci of systematic theology. The reader may note that such categories as angelology (the doctrine of angels) have not been addressed, while others such as soteriology (the doctrine of salvation) have been interwoven into chapters addressing other issues. Our purpose has not been to treat every fountainhead of doctrine but to model how a Christian may approach an area of theology and derive its necessary missiological implications. Other subjects, such as the identity of the *ethne* in the Great Commission or the character of a pastor-theologian as derived from the Epistles, have been given more attention in this volume as they represent dimensions of ecclesiology vital to missions. Though these themes are not often the subject of strict systematic theological treatment, we hold that one's missiology should be informed not only by one's systematic theology but also by such disciplines as biblical and pastoral theology.

What unifies this entire project has been our aim of applying the explicit instructions of Scripture to missions in such a way as to *regulate* and not merely *norm* the missionary task. As mentioned at the onset, this regulative principle maintains that *only* and *all that* Scripture prescribes—regarding public worship, missions, pastoral ministry, or any other task entrusted to the church—is to be adopted as official practice by the people of God. This principle is often misunderstood as placing undue restriction on churches without adequately considering the unique cultural circumstances in which they are found. This is an error. The positive instructions set forward in Scripture are both liberating in their simplicity and surprisingly lenient in what they allow. Consider how the Puritan theologian John Owen expressed this regulative principle in its application to the local church assembly:

> It is now otherwise with the people of God, be they never so poor, and destitute of all outward accommodations. Are their assemblies in the mountains, in the caves and dens of the earth?—Christ, according to his promise, is in the midst of them as their high priest, and they have in their worship all the order, glory, and beauty (I mean, observing gospel rules) that in any place under heaven they can enjoy and be made partakers of. All depends on the presence of Christ, and their access to God by him; and he is excluded from no place, but thinks any place adorned sufficiently for him which his

saints are met in or driven unto. Let the hands that hang down be lifted up, and feeble knees be strengthened;—whatever their outward, distressed condition may be, here is order, beauty, and glory, in the worship of God, above all that the world can pretend unto![1]

The principle, stated differently, is this: when the church has the living, powerful, spiritual, and real presence of the Lord Jesus Christ in its midst by his Spirit and the simple, sufficient, ordinary means of grace at its disposal, the church has all it needs. The people of God can worship authentically in cathedrals or caves and lack nothing necessary for life and godliness (2 Peter 1:3). Such biblical worship possesses a subversively simple glory—lacking the extravagance of outward forms boasted by Old Testament worship or even the modern worship-as-entertainment experience but possessing far greater spiritual power.[2] Similarly, the people of God have everything they need to discharge the mission of God if they possess Scripture, sound doctrine, and the power of the Spirit—even if they lack the specialized expertise necessary to catalyze social movements. This is because healthy missiology is to flow out of theology rather than be artificially appended to it.

Modeling our missionary practice according to the express regulations of Scripture in no way places us at enmity with aims and practices such as building redemptive relationships with nationals, conducting evangelistic Bible studies with unbelievers, prayerfully seeking to convert entire households and social units, conducting church more secretively in closed countries, placing a strong emphasis on indigenization, or encouraging every-member ministry and missional living among

---

1 John Owen, *The Works of John Owen*, ed. William H. Goold (Edinburgh: Banner of Truth, 1965), 9:66–67.

2 Note WCF (1647) 7.6 on this point: "Under the gospel, when Christ, the substance, was exhibited, the ordinances in which this covenant is dispensed are the preaching of the Word, and the administration of the sacraments of Baptism and the Lord's Supper: which, though fewer in number, and administered with more simplicity, and less outward glory; yet, in them, it is held forth in more fulness, evidence, and spiritual efficacy, to all nations." Though most Baptists object to the "one covenant, multiple administrations" articulation of covenant theology on which this line of the confession depends, the underlying observation concerning the glory of new covenant worship, despite the apparent simplicity of its outward forms, stands.

laypersons. These common elements of contemporary missiology are often placed in opposition to the so-called proclamational methodology. Such tension is false and artificial. A missionary operating on the basis of clear biblical regulation may be able to make liberal use of such strategies when contextually appropriate. Even the Second London Confession of Faith, which many modern missiologists would perhaps disparage as reflecting a purely Western model of Christian practice, acknowledges the clear necessity of healthy contextualization in domains of life in which Scripture provides minimal guidance: "There are some circumstances concerning the worship of God, and government of the church, common to human actions and societies, *which are to be ordered by the light of nature and Christian prudence, according to the general rules of the Word*, which are always to be observed."[3]

This means that even within what the contemporary missions community would marginalize with descriptors such as "Western," "traditional," or "proclamational," there exists a necessary appreciation for contextual considerations—culture, language, time, and place—which fall into the domain of wisdom. We long to see this wonderful synthesis of biblical regulation, wisdom, and conscience bear fruit on the mission field. But this cannot happen until we see the missionary task first and foremost as a *theological* endeavor.

A closing anecdote will serve to illustrate our purpose throughout this work. As we neared completion of this manuscript, one of the authors conversed with a young woman at church and described the book's aim to her. As soon as the woman—a faithful, biblically literate believer—heard that the topic was missions, with wide-eyed interest, she responded, "I don't know anything about missions. I've always wanted to understand it." Her humility is commendable. Would that more young adults in our generation recognize the borders of their expertise! Yet the notion that a vibrant, Scripture-saturated adult follower of Christ in a Bible-teaching church would think herself unequipped to weigh matters relating to the Great Commission represents a failure of the collective evangelical missions establishment. And this woman

---

3 2LCF (1689) 1.6, emphasis added.

is not alone—even many well-trained pastors feel equally ill-equipped in this realm.

How did this happen? Simply put, missions has become siloed from the rest of the life of the church as something *other*, a distinct discipline in its own right, of a different essence from the regular ministry of Word and sacrament that marks Christian community where it is already established. This growing divide has occurred alongside the infusion of sociology, anthropology, psychology, economics, and even politics into missions, requiring of its practitioners a level of academic qualification unattainable by laymen. In the name of catalyzing organic gospel movements, we have widened the once-unacceptable divide between the laity and clergy by making missions something it is biblically *not*—an independent enterprise severed from the local church. Consequently, pastors and laymen, conditioned to doubt the sufficiency of Scripture for cross-cultural ministry, now approach "professional missionaries" and missions work with fear and trepidation.

To correct this alarming trend, the missions community abroad and church leaders in positions of influence as senders must together embrace an unpopular truth: if one must become an expert in social movements or growth strategies, as defined by secular sociology, to be faithful as a missionary, then whatever it is we are practicing cannot rightly be called biblical missions. We can accept this truth while still recognizing that missions requires specialized skills that not all believers possess—from the ability to master one or more foreign languages and weather culture shock to entrepreneurial instincts and cultural sensitivity. We do not deny the uniqueness of missions, nor do we affirm in an overly simplistic manner that every Christian is a missionary. In fact, relatively few Christians are ordained to gospel work among a people group different from their own. But our driving motivation with this volume is to demystify missions and thereby open it up to ordinary, Spirit-filled, Bible-reading Christians. Missions is *not* of a different essence from the sort of gospel ministry that we pray is practiced in our own churches. Relocation, contextualization, translation, and enculturation all serve to set the stage for the missionary to boldly and simply proclaim Christ and him crucified in such a way as to be understood through the static of his hearers' conflicting worldviews, whether he is met with acceptance or rejection. The aim of missionary strategy is never to shift the missionary enterprise away from the simplicity of gospel proclamation or to circumvent the necessary offense of the gospel. Missions is more than simply proclaiming the gospel; but it is absolutely *never* less. This is a difficult and high calling, but it need not be dauntingly *complex*.

Our risen and reigning Lord entrusted his missionary mandate to his bride, the church, and not merely to the world of parachurch organizations and academics that were to someday emerge. We aim to place the Great Commission back into the hands of the local church. Bible in hand, any faithful Christian disciple can make sense of the task of missions in such a way as to faithfully and confidently pray, give, send, or go. The more we do missions by the Book, the more we can return missions to the local church as its proper steward. And only in so doing will we see all the nations won to the obedience of faith in the Lamb, who is worthy to receive the glorious reward of his sufferings.

APPENDIX

THE APOSTOLIC EVANGELISTIC PREACHING PATTERN

These charts are adapted by Joel Heppner from the work of Alan J. Thompson, *The Acts of the Risen Lord Jesus: Luke's Account of God's Unfolding Plan*, ed. D. A. Carson, New Studies in Biblical Theology (England: Apollos; Downers Grove, IL: InterVarsity Press, 2011), 27:90. We are deeply indebted to these scholars for their careful work.

Gospel Preaching Pattern

Sermon	Acts 2	Acts 3	Acts 4	Acts 5	Acts 10	Acts 13	Acts 17
The Occasion	2:12–13 (cf. 2:1–11)	3:11 (cf. 3:1–10)	4:5–7 (cf. 4:1–3)	5:27–28 (cf. 5:12–26)	10:30–33 (cf. 10:1–29)	13:13–15	17:16–21
The Audience	2:5	3:11	4:5–6	5:27	10:27 (10:24)	13:13–15	17:22
Apostolic Preacher	2:14	3:12	4:1, 7–8	5:29	10:34	13:16	17:22
Begins with God	2:16–17	3:13	4:19	5:29–30	10:34, 36	13:16–23	17:22–29
Gospel Events	2:22–23	3:13–15	4:10–11, 20	5:30–31	10:36–42	13:23–37	17:31
2 Primary Benefits	2:38 (2:21, 40)	3:16, 19, 21, 25–26	4:12	5:31–32	10:42–43 (10:44, 11:15–18)	13:38–39, 46, 48	17:30–31
Required Response	2:38, 41	3:16–26	4:12 (Implied cf. 3:16–26)	5:31–32	10:43, 47–48 (11:17–18)	13:39, 48	17:30 (17:34)

Sermon	Acts 2	Acts 3	Acts 4	Acts 5	Acts 10	Acts 13	Acts 17
The Occasion	Pentecost, response to speaking in tongues	Walk to temple, encounter a lame man	Arrest by Sadducees	Sadducees arrest apostles	Peter sent to Cornelius	Paul's journey to Antioch in Pisidia	Paul in Athens
The Audience	Jews from every nation	People gathered in Solomon's Portico	Rulers, elders, scribes, high priestly family	The council and high priest	Cornelius and his household, relatives, and friends	Local synagogue	Epicurean and Stoic philosophers
Apostolic Preacher	Peter	Peter	Peter	Peter & the apostles	Peter	Paul	Paul
Begins with God	God's work in the last day	The God of our fathers	Jesus Christ healed, God raised Jesus from the dead	Obey God rather than men, God raised & exalted Jesus	God sent Jesus to preach and heal	God rescued Israel from Egypt, God's work in Israel	God who made the world and everything in it
Gospel Events	Life & miracles, death, resurrection & exaltation	Glorification of Jesus by suffering and death and resurrection	Crucifixion & resurrection, rejected by men	Hung on tree, resurrection & exaltation	Jesus preaches, baptized, hung on a tree, raised	Jesus tried and condemned, dead, buried, raised, appeared	Jesus will judge, raised from the dead
2 Primary Benefits	Salvation, forgiveness & Holy Spirit	Blot our sins, restore all things	Salvation	Forgiveness of sins, Holy Spirit	Forgiveness of sins, Holy Spirit	Forgiveness of sins	Assurance of salvation at judgment
Required Response	Repent & be baptized	Repent, listen to Christ	Trust in Jesus, implied faith & repentance	Repentance & obedience	Believe, baptism	Belief in Christ	Repent, believe

Bibliography

Aquinas, Thomas. *Commentary on the Gospel of John: Chapters 1–21.* Translated by Fabian Larcher and James A. Weisheipl. Vol. 3. Washington, DC: The Catholic University of America Press, 2010.

Augustine. "Exposition on Psalm 43.4." *Expositions on the Psalms.* https://www.newadvent.org/fathers/1801043.htm.

"The Bond of the Missionary Brotherhood of Serampore, 1805." In George Smith, *The Life of William Carey, D.D., Shoemaker and Missionary,* 442–456. Edinburgh: R. & R. Clark, 1885.

Buser, Brad. "Church Planting Movement Model vs the Proclamational Model." *Radius International* (blog). December 17, 2018. https://www.radiusinternational.org/church-planting-movement-model-and-the-proclamational-model-debate.

Calvin, John. *Institutes of the Christian Religion.* Translated by Henry Beveridge. Grand Rapids: Eerdmans, 1989. Accessed August 26, 2020. https://www.ccel.org/ccel/calvin/institutes/institutes.vi.xv.html.

Calvin, John. *Sermons on Second Timothy.* Carlisle, PA: Banner of Truth, 2018.

Calvin, John and Jacopo Sadoleto. *A Reformation Debate.* Edited by John C. Olin. Grand Rapids: Baker Publishing Group, 1966.

Calvin, John and Matthew Henry. *1, 2, & 3 John.* Crossway Classic Commentaries. Wheaton, IL: Crossway, 1998.

Carey, Eustace. *Memoir of William Carey, D.D.: Late Missionary to Bengal; Professor of Oriental Languages in the College of Fort William, Calcutta.* Boston: Gould, Kendall and Lincoln, 1836.

Carlson, Darren and Elliot Clark. "The 3 Words That Changed Missions Strategy—and Why We Might Be Wrong." *The Gospel Coalition*. September 11, 2019. https://www.thegospelcoalition.org/article/misleading-words-missions-strategy-unreached-people-groups.

Catechism of the Catholic Church. Accessed January 2, 2021. https://www.vatican.va/archive/ccc_css/archive/catechism/p123a9p4.htm.

Chung, Sun Young and Todd M. Johnson. "Tracking Global Christianity's Statistical Centre of Gravity, AD 33–AD 2100." *International Review of Mission* 95 (2004): 166–181, cited in John Morgan. "World Christianity Is Undergoing a Seismic Shift." *ABWE Blog*. ABWE International, June 27, 2019. https://www.abwe.org/blog/world-christianity-undergoing-seismic-shift.

Cyprian. *On the Unity of the Church*. Translated by Robert Ernest Wallis. From *Ante-Nicene Fathers*, Vol. 5. Edited by Alexander Roberts, James Donaldson, and A. Cleveland Coxe. Buffalo, NY: Christian Literature, 1886. Revised and edited for New Advent by Kevin Knight. http://www.newadvent.org/fathers/050701.htm.

Dunford, Scott and Alex Kocman. "Serving Christ in Suffering: Jenn DeKryger on Togo and the Loss of Todd DeKryger." August 27, 2018. *The Missions Podcast*. Podcast. https://missionspodcast.com/podcast/serving-christ-in-suffering-jenn-dekryger-on-togo-and-the-loss-of-todd-dekryger.

Esler, Ted. "Coming to Terms: Two Church Planting Paradigms." *International Journal of Frontier Missiology* 30, no. 2 (Summer 2013). https://www.ijfm.org/PDFs_IJFM/30_2_PDFs/IJFM_30_2-Esler.pdf.

FranklinCovey. "Habit 2: Begin with the End in Mind." Accessed October 10, 2020. https://www.franklincovey.com/the-7-habits/habit-2.

"A Friendly Debate: Session 1 'Who Is God?'" Filmed February 24, 2020 at Laurelglen Bible Church. Video, 2:30:03. https://vimeo.com/390870064.

Georges, Jayson. *The 3D Gospel: Ministry in Guilt, Shame, and Fear Cultures*. Timē Press, 2014.

Georges, Jayson. "Improving Anselm's Atonement Theory." *HonorShame* (blog). December 2, 2015. http://honorshame.com/improving-anselms-atonement-theory.

Georges, Jayson and Mark D. Baker. *Ministering in Honor-Shame Cultures: Biblical Foundations and Practical Essentials*. Downers Grove: IVP Academic, 2016.

Gilbert, Greg. *What Is the Gospel?* Wheaton: Crossway, 2010.

Gill, Brad. "AM Service—Missions Conference Speaker." Sermon. First Baptist Church of St. Johns, MI. March 22, 2015. MP3 audio, 46:06. http://stjohnsfbc.com/sermons.html.

Gill, Brad. "A Christology for Frontier Mission: A Missiological Study of Colossians." *International Journal of Frontier Missiology*, no. 34 (2017): 93–102.

Gill, John. *An Exposition of the New Testament*. The Baptist Commentary Series. London: Mathews and Leigh, 1809.

Gravelle, Gilles. "Short-Term Missions & Money." Moving Missions. 2012. movingmissions.org/wp-content/pdfs/short-term-missions-and-money.pdf.

Harriman, David. "Force Majeure: Ethics and Encounters in an Era of Extreme Contextualization." In *Muslim Conversions to Christ*, edited by Ayman Ibrahim and Ant Greenham, 455–500. New York: Peter Lang, 2018.

Harward, Naomi. "Don't Waste Your Grief." *Message Magazine*, July 2018.

Hinn, Costi W. and Anthony G. Wood. *Defining Deception: Freeing the Church from the Mystical-Miracle Movement*. El Cajon: Southern California Seminary Press, 2018.

Hodge, Charles. *An Exposition of the Second Epistle to the Corinthians*. New York: A. C. Armstrong & Son, 1891.

Ignatius. "The Epistle of Ignatius to the Romans." Translated by Alexander Roberts and James Donaldson. In vol. 1 of *Ante-Nicene Fathers*, edited by Alexander Roberts, James Donaldson, and A. Cleveland Coxe. Buffalo, NY: Christian Literature, 1885. Revised and edited by Kevin Knight for New Advent, http://www.newadvent.org/fathers/0107.htm.

IMB Global Research 2020. "People Groups." Accessed September 2, 2020. http://peoplegroups.org.

Jillette, Penn. "A Gift of a Bible." July 8, 2010. Video, 5:11. https://www.youtube.com/watch?v=6md638smQd8.

Joshua Project. "Joshua Project." Frontier Ventures. Accessed January 2, 2021. https://joshuaproject.net.

Kocman, Alex. "3 Reasons Definite Atonement is Basic to Biblical Missions." Founders Ministries, January 21, 2019. https://founders.org/2019/01/21/3-reasons-definite-atonement-is-basic-to-biblical-missions.

Kocman, Alex. "What Should We Do With 'Persons of Peace'?" *ABWE Blog*. ABWE International, October 2, 2019. https://www.abwe.org/blog/what-should-we-do-%E2%80%98persons-peace%E2%80%99.

Lewis, Rebecca. "Insider Movements: Retaining Identity and Preserving Community." In *Perspectives on the World Christian Movement*, edited by Ralph Winter and Steven Hawthorne, 4th ed. 673–676. Pasadena, CA: William Carey, 2009.

Machen, J. Gresham. *Christianity and Liberalism*. Grand Rapids: Eerdmans, 1923.

Mallouhi, Mazhar, ed. *The True Meaning of the Gospel and Acts in Arabic*. Beirut, Lebanon: Dar Al Farabi, 2008.

Muller, Roland. *Honor and Shame: Unlocking the Door*. Bloomington, IN: Xlibris, 2001.

Murray, Iain H. *Revival and Revivalism*. Edinburgh: Banner of Truth, 1994.

Murray, John. *Redemption Accomplished and Applied*. Grand Rapids: Eerdmans, 2015.

Nazianzen, Gregory. "Select Orations of Saint Gregory Nazianzen." In *S. Cyril of Jerusalem, S. Gregory Nazianzen*, edited by Philip Schaff and Henry Wace, translated by Charles Gordon Browne and James Edward Swallow. Vol. 7 of *A Select Library of the Nicene and Post-Nicene Fathers of the Christian Church, Second Series*. New York: Christian Literature Company, 1894.

Owen, John. *The Works of John Owen*. Edited by William Henry Goold. 16 vols. Edinburgh: Banner of Truth Trust, 1965.

Piper, John. "Abortion and the Narrow Way That Leads to Life." Sermon. Bethlehem Baptist Church. January 23, 2011. Minneapolis, MN. Transcript, audio, video, 41:24. https://www.desiringgod.org/messages/abortion-and-the-narrow-way-that-leads-to-life.

Piper, John. *Let the Nations Be Glad! The Supremacy of God in Missions*. 3rd ed. Grand Rapids: Baker Academic, 2010.

Skinker, Loren. "All Things for Good." *Message Magazine*, July 2020.

Stanley, Andy. "Aftermath, Part 3: Not Difficult // Andy Stanley." Filmed April 2018 in Alpharetta, Georgia. Video, 39:44. https://www.youtube.com/watch?v=pShxFTNRCWI.

Strayer, Hannah. "How One African Went From Shouting the Muslim Call to Prayer to Sharing the Call of Christ." *ABWE Blog*. ABWE International, January 15, 2020. https://www.abwe.org/blog/how-one-african-went-shouting-muslim-call-prayer-sharing-call-christ.

Synod of Dort (1618–1619). *The Canons of Dort*. Pensacola: Chapel Library, 2010. https://www.chapellibrary.org:8443/pdf/books/codo.pdf.

Thompson, Alan J. *The Acts of the Risen Lord Jesus: Luke's Account of God's Unfolding Plan*. New Studies in Biblical Theology. Vol. 27. Edited by D. A. Carson. Downers Grove, IL: InterVarsity Press, 2011.

Traveling Team, The. "Missions Stats: The Current State of the World." Accessed September 19, 2020. http://www.thetravelingteam.org/stats.

Travis, John [pseud.]. "The C1–C6 Spectrum: A Practical Tool for Defining Six Types of 'Christ-Centered Communities' Found in the Muslim Context." In *Perspectives on the World Christian Movement*. Edited by Ralph Winter and Steven Hawthorne. 4th ed. 664–665. Pasadena, CA: William Carey, 2009.

Trousdale, Jerry. *Miraculous Movements: How Hundreds of Thousands of Muslims are Falling in Love with Jesus*. Nashville: Thomas Nelson, 2012.

Tyndale, William. *The Works of William Tyndale*. Vol. 1. 1848. Reprint, Edinburgh, Scotland: Banner of Truth, 2010.

United Bible Societies. "About Us: Incredible Growth in Scripture Translation." UBS Translations. 2008. http://www.ubs-translations.org/about_us.

van Mastricht, Petrus. *Prolegomena*. Translated by Todd M. Rester. Edited by Joel R. Beeke. Vol. 1 of *Theoretical-Practical Theology*. Grand Rapids: Reformation Heritage Books, 2018.

Vegas, Chad. "A Brief Guide to DMM." *Radius International* (blog). June 11, 2018. https://www.radiusinternational.org/a-brief-guide-to-dmm/.

Vegas, Chad. "The Ultimate Injustice: Gospel Privilege and Global Missions." In Jared Longshore, ed., *By What Standard*, 137–151. Cape Coral, FL: Founders, 2020.

Wagner, Roger. *Tongues Aflame: Learning to Preach from the Apostles*. Fearn, UK: Christian Focus, 2004.

Wallace, Daniel B. *Greek Grammar beyond the Basics: An Exegetical Syntax of the New Testament*. Grand Rapids: Zondervan, 1996.

Winter, Ralph. "Three Mission Eras and the Loss and Recovery of Kingdom Mission, 1800–2000." In *Perspectives on the World Christian Movement*, edited by Ralph Winter and Steven Hawthorne, 4th ed. 263–278. Pasadena, CA: William Carey, 2009.

Winter, Ralph. "Unreached Peoples: The Development of the Concept." *International Journal of Frontier Missions* 1, no. 2 (1984): 131.

Winter, Ralph and Bruce A. Koch. "Finishing the Task: The Unreached Peoples Challenge." In *Perspectives on the World Christian Movement*. Edited by Ralph Winter and Steven Hawthorne. 4th ed. 531–546. Pasadena, CA: William Carey, 2009.

Wu, Jackson. *Reading Romans with Eastern Eyes: Honor and Shame in Paul's Message and Mission*. Downers Grove, IL: InterVarsity Press, 2019.

Scripture Index

Old Testament

Genesis

1:26–28	24
1:28	62
1:31	130
3:15	37, 60, 114
11:4	62
12:1–3	91
12:2	98
12:2	98n13
12:3	40, 62, 97

Numbers

23:19	15
22	53

Deuteronomy

4:6–8	62, 91
6:4	23
6:4–9	25
7:6	62
23:1–2, 8	64
29:29	69, 128
32:8	98n13

1 Samuel

16:7	98

2 Samuel

7:12–13	33
7:16	71

Ezra

7:10	139

Nehemiah

8:1–8	64
8:8	139
13:1	64

Psalm

2:1–3	34
2:4	36
2:4–6	36, 37
2:6	37
2:7–9	23, 38
2:8	40
2:10	41
2:10–12	41
2:12	42
14:1–3	34
16:10–11	72
19:1	13
19:7	14
22:27	95
46:10	123
51:5	34
67	91
67:3–5	63
96:3	63
110:1	38
110:1–2	39
119:71	122

Isaiah	
11:9	62, 95
32:15	80
43:7	62
53:5	36
55:11	18
56:7	63
64:4	132
66	92
66:12, 18–20	98

Ezekiel	
18:23	94

Daniel	
2:35	71
7:13–14	23, 40

Joel	
2:28–32	80

Habakkuk	
1:13	34
2:14	62, 95, 130

New Testament

Matthew

5:2–12	136
5:43–48	29
6:23	67
6:26–33	29
7:14	93
9:38	104
10:38	120
11:25–27	115
12:30	93
16:13–19	65
16:17	69
16:18	57, 71
16:19	69
17:5	38
18:12–13	94
18:17	65, 70
18:20	65
22:31	18
24:36	128
26:64	40
28:17–20	23
28:18	31, 32
28:18–19	38
28:18–20	23
28:19	10n5, 41, 47, 68, 79, 98
28:19–20	94
28:20	23, 91

Mark

11:17	98
14:62	40

Luke

1:33	71
1:41–43	52
1:67–69	52
2:25–32	52
3:22	38
4:5–7	40
4:16	64
6:13	78
10:2	104
10:6–7	140n3
14:25–33	143
14:26–33	120
16:19–31	92
24:17	18
24:44–46	77, 114n4
24:44–47	79
24:44–49	80
24:45	77
24:45–47	18
24:46–47	51, 80
24:46–49	75
24:47	77, 82
24:47–48	50, 77
24:47–49	50, 51, 54
24:48	79
24:48–49	77
24:49	45, 49, 50, 77, 83

John

1:1	34
1:14	34, 114
1:18	114
3:1–8	50
3:8:24	92
3:16	21, 25
3:17	25, 91, 129
3:17–21	25
3:35	39
3:36	92
4:42	25
5:23	42
5:28, 29	129
5:39	14
6:37	42
6:44	69

10:30	34	3:13–16	81
11:25	37	3:17–26	81
12:31	36, 40	3:20–21	80
14:6	42, 93	4:12	93
14:16–17	23, 138	4:23–31	33
14:16–17, 23	50	4:24–28	25
14:19	37	4:27	34
14:23	23, 138	4:31	33, 52
14:26	54	10:34	81
15:26	49	11:19–20	97
15:26–16:15	52	13:1–3	73
15:26–27	50, 54	14:21	101
16:7	48	14:21–22	101
16:7–11	50	14:23	73, 78, 101
16:7–15	54	16:6	94
16:12–15	50	16:30–31	80
16:14–15	50	17:2	83
17:1–5	23	17:3	83
20:21	72	17:24–25	81
20:23	67	17:26–31	81
20:28	66	17:28	24
		20:7	65
		20:17–21	141, 143
		20:17–35	78
		20:28–31	85, 141, 143
		24:15	129
		28:25–28	94

Acts

1:3	80
1:4–5	50
1:8	50, 51, 54, 77, 79, 83, 95
1:9	38
1:11	128
1:14	64
1:15–26	78
2:4:8–12	52
2:5–47	52
2:11	83
2:23	35
2:24	37
2:33	38, 77
2:36	37
2:37–38	80
2:38, 41–42	68
2:41	70
2:42	139
2:42–47	64
3:13	80

Romans

1:4–5	87
1:5	51, 89
1:6	69
1:8–32	22
1:16	53, 140
1:16:25–27	51
1:16	109n2
1:18–31	26
1:20	13
2:14–15	13, 98
3:9–11	27
3:9–20	26
3:9–26	22
3:10–11	34

3:25–26	35	2:9	132
4:25	37	2:10–14	50, 53
5:3–4	123	4:9–13	121
5:5	50	5:4–5	65, 70
5:8	25	5:12–13	70
5:10	38	8:6	24
5:12	34	9:16	89
5:12–21	40	9:24–27	142
5:17	37	11:26	69
6:23	26	12:3	50, 53
8:7	35	12:11	103
8:9–15	50	15:1–3	139
8:15	50	15:1–11	80
8:15–17	50	15:17	37
8:18	122	15:21–23	129
8:21	129	15:22–23	37
8:26–27	50	15:23	72
8:28–29	29, 123	15:24	130
8:34	38	15:24–25	41
9:18–24	94	15:24–27	38
10:9–13	36	15:58	130
10:9–15	92	16:2	65
10:13	93		
10:14–15	84, 93	**2 Corinthians**	
10:14–17	115	1:8–9	126
10:17	12	2:1–5	111
11:7–8	113	2:14	18
15:16	100	2:14–17	110
15:19, 23	94	2:16	111
15:20	101	2:17	6, 111
15:21	101	3:4–6	111, 138
17–21	101	3:5	117
		3:6–9	111
1 Corinthians		3:18	50
1:17	6, 111	4:1–2	6, 110, 144
1:17; 2:5	110	4:1–6	109n2
1:18	18, 112	4:2	112
2:1–5	6, 109, 140	4:3–4	113
2:1–5	109n2	4:5–6	114
2:1–14	115, 117	4:6	114
2:2	114	4:7	52, 107, 115
2:3–5	124	4:7–12	110, 126
2:5	115	4:8–10	120

4:13	14	2:4–5	26
4:14	126	2:8	1
4:15	124	2:10	137
4:16–18	121	2:11–12	98
4:17	119	2:20	52, 78, 139
5:1–5	125	3:6	63
5:6	126	4:7–16	85
5:8	72	4:8–10	72
5:11–21	138	4:11–16	139
5:14	29	4:24	62
5:17	51, 114	5:1–2	29
5:18–21	114	5:25–27	37
5:21	35	6:17	16, 19
10:4–6	38		
10:10–12	110	Philippians	
10:11:12–15	110	2:7	34
11:12–15	6	3:21	129
11:23–29	121		
11:30–12:11	110	Colossians	
12:12	78	1:12	vii
12:12	109n2	1:13–14	60
13:14	50	1:20	91
		1:23	99
Galatians		1:24	124, 141
1:6–9	85, 139	1:28	41
1:6–10	112	1:28–29	115, 143
1:8	18	2:14–15	36
1:11–16	110	3:1–4	50, 143
2:10	130	3:10	62
4:4	34	4:3–4	112
4:4–6	50		
5:22	29	1 Thessalonians	
		2:13	52
Ephesians			
1:3–6	26, 138	2 Thessalonians	
1:3–14	110	1:5, 7–9	129
1:7–12	49, 138		
1:11	60	1 Timothy	
1:13–14	49, 50, 138	1:2–3	137
1:16–18	50	1:3	103
2:1–3	26	1:15	36
2:1–9	109n2		

2:4	94
3:1–12	78
3:16	99
4:6–16	136
4:6, 16	137
4:11–15	145
4:12	137, 140
4:13	19, 140
4:13–14	137
4:16	142, 144
6:12–13	67

2 Timothy

1:2–5	137
1:8	138, 141
1:8–10	137
1:9	39
1:11–14	138
1:13	85, 139, 140, 142
1:14	85, 138, 139, 142
1:15	137
2:1	137
2:2	73, 139, 146
2:3	141
2:3–6	142
2:5	146
2:7	135, 143
2:10	124
2:15	22, 140, 143
2:19	65
3:14–16	139
3:15	14
3:16	7, 9, 14, 15, 52
3:17	7, 9, 15
4:1–2	82
4:1–4	139
4:1–5	143
4:7–8	142
19–21	16

Titus

1:2	15, 39
1:5–9	78
1:9	140, 142
1:9–16	85
2:14	60
3:5	50

Hebrews

1:1–2	14, 28, 39, 114n4
1:3	34
2:4	78
4:12	16, 19
4:14–16	36
4:15	34
10:19–22	36
10:24–25	65
10:32–39	136
11:6	92
12:2	122

James

1:18	19
1:27	131
2:1	98
2:2	64

1 Peter

1:1–2	69
1:1–8	51
1:10–12	14, 15
1:23	19
2:2	19
2:9	62, 63

2 Peter

1:3	16
1:3–4	14
1:19–21	139
1:21	14
3:9	41, 94

1 John

2:23	34, 93
3:2	129

3:8	37
4:8	21, 25
4:9–10	26
4:16	25

3 John

5–8	29, 30

Revelation

1:5	37
1:9	126
1:10	65
2:1	65
2:10	127
5:9	11, 60, 62, 96
5:9–10	100
6:16	42
7:9	11, 127
7:14	127
12:11	38, 127
19:7–9	37
21:4	127

About the Authors

Chad Vegas is the founding pastor of Sovereign Grace Church of Bakersfield, the founding board chairman of Radius International and Radius Theological Institute, and the founding board vice-chairman of Providence Classical Academy. He also serves as adjunct faculty for IRBS Theological Seminary and the Institute of Public Theology. He has been married to Teresa since 1994 and has two children.

Alex Kocman is the director of advancement and communications for Association of Baptists for World Evangelism (ABWE) and cohosts The Missions Podcast weekly. Previously he served in mobilization with ABWE, as an instructor in apologetics for Liberty University Online, and as a student pastor. Alex's writing has been featured on Founders Ministries, 9Marks, For the Church, and more. He serves on staff at Faith Bible Fellowship Church in York, Pennsylvania, where he resides with his wife Hanna and three children.

Other Titles from Founders Press

BY WHAT STANDARD? God's World . . . God's Rules.
Edited by Jared Longshore

> I'm grateful for the courage of these men and the clarity of their voices. This is a vitally important volume, sounding all the right notes of passion, warning, instruction, and hope.
>
> —Phil Johnson, Executive Director,
> Grace To You

Truth & Grace Memory Books
Edited by Thomas K. Ascol

> Memorizing a good, age-appropriate catechism is as valuable for learning the Bible as memorizing multiplication tables is for learning mathematics.
>
> —Dr. Don Whitney, Professor,
> The Southern Baptist Theological Seminary

Dear Timothy: Letters on Pastoral Ministry
Edited by Thomas K. Ascol

> Get this book. So many experienced pastors have written in this book it is a gold mine of wisdom for young pastors in how to preach and carry out their ministerial life.
>
> —Joel Beeke, President,
> Puritan Reformed Theological Seminary

The Mystery of Christ, His Covenant & His Kingdom
By Samuel Renihan

> This book serves for an excellent and rich primer on covenant theology and demonstrates how it leads from the Covenant of Redemption to the final claiming and purifying of the people given by the Father to the Son.
>
> —Tom Nettles, Retired Professor of Historical Theology,
> The Southern Baptist Theological Seminary

Strong And Courageous: Following Jesus Amid the Rise of America's New Religion
By Tom Ascol and Jared Longshore

> We have had quite enough of "Be Nice and Inoffensive." We are overflowing with "Be Tolerant and Sensitive." It is high time that we were admonished to "Be Strong and Courageous."
>
> —Jim Scott Orrick, Author, Pastor of Bullitt Lick Baptist Church

ADDITIONAL TITLES

Still Confessing: An Exposition of the Baptist Faith & Message 2000
By Daniel Scheiderer

By His Grace and for His Glory
By Tom Nettles

Getting the Garden Right
By Richard C. Barcellos

The Law and the Gospel
By Ernie Reisinger

Traditional Theology & the SBC
By Tom Ascol

Teaching Truth, Training Hearts
By Tom Nettles

Heirs of the Reformation: A Study in Baptist Origins
By Daniel Scheiderer

COMING IN 2021

Praise Is His Gracious Choice:
Corporate Worship Expressing Biblical Truth
By Dr. Tom Nettles

Just Thinking: about the state
By Darrell Harrison and Virgil Walker

The Transcultural Gospel
By E.D. Burns

Ancient Gospel, Brave New World
By E.D. Burns

Galatians: He Did It All
By Baruch Maoz

Baptist Symbolics Vol. 1
For the Vindication of the Truth: A Brief Exposition of the
First London Baptist Confession of Faith
By James M. Renihan

Order these titles and more at press.founders.org